BBC goodfood
TRAYBAKES

D1353901

10 9 8

BBC Books, an imprint of Ebury Publishing
20 Vauxhall Bridge Road,
London SW1V 2SA

BBC Books is part of the Penguin Random House
group of companies whose addresses can
be found at global.penguinrandomhouse.com

Penguin
Random House
UK

Photographs © BBC Worldwide 2014
Recipes © BBC Worldwide 2014
Book design © Woodlands Books Ltd 2014
All recipes contained in this book first
appeared in BBC *Good Food* magazine.

First published by BBC Books in 2014

www.eburypublishing.co.uk

A CIP catalogue record for this book
is available from the British Library

ISBN 9781849907842

Printed and bound in China by Toppan Leefung

Project editor: Lizzy Gaisford
Designer: Kathryn Gammon
Cover Design: Interstate Creative Partners Ltd
Production: Alex Goddard
Picture Researcher: Gabby Harrington

PICTURE AND RECIPE CREDITS

BBC *Good Food* magazine and BBC Books would
like to thank the following people for providing
photos. While every effort has been made to
trace and acknowledge all photographers,
we should like to apologise should there be
any errors or omissions.

Marie-Louise Avery p117, p199; Peter Cassidy
p25, p123, p129, p187; Jean Cazals p27, p191;
Will Heap p79, p95, p121, p125, p143, p171, p179,
p193; Lara Holmes p49; Jonathan Kennedy p53;
p157 Gareth Morgans p29, p85, p87, p91, p135,
p139, p195, p209; David Munns p39, p45, p65,
p67, p77, p81, p93, p97, p101, p103, p131, p139,
p147, p151, p155, p181, p203; Myles New p11, p13,
p63, p47, p51, p55, p57, p59, p61, p69, p107, p109,
p111, p145, p159, p163, p183, p201, p207;
Stuart Ovenden p23, p33, p35, p71, p113, p141,
p177; Lis Parsons p19, p31, p41, p83, p89, p105,
p115, p133, p115, p161, p169, p197; Maja Smend
p119, p167; Simon Smith p43, p73, p137, p149;
Sam Stowell p175, p185, p205; Philip Webb p17,
p37, p153, p165, p189; Jon Whitaker p21;
Elizabeth Zeschin p99, p199

All the recipes in this book were created by the
editorial team at *Good Food* and by regular
contributors to BBC Magazines.

goodfood
TRAYBAKES

EDITOR
Sarah Cook

BOOKS

Contents

Introduction

Baking really is the new rock and roll, and nothing puts a smile on a face quite like a slice of homemade cake.

Let's forget the buns, bundts and babas, we're here to celebrate the traybake – and this little book will show you just how creative you can be with only a couple of everyday tins that you've probably already got stashed in a cupboard somewhere!

Perfectly portion-able and ideal for batch-baking, traybakes will probably become the most versatile method of cooking in your repertoire. We've a whole chapter full of simple, kid-friendly favourites so you can get your little ones into the kitchen with you, and another packed with super-special ideas that are bound to wow friends and family on birthdays and bake-offs. If you're a bit of a chocoholic, not to worry, we've flapjacks, bars and brownies to keep you happy. And for those occasions when something savoury is more appropriate, there are plenty of options, from chunky cornbread, to a naughty but nice full English frittata that will make any picnic memorable.

There really isn't an occasion for which we don't have a traybake – cover them in frosting and sprinkles and you've got a sponge that will fly off a charity cake stall. Roll them up and you've got a gorgeous roulade like our scrummy Peach melba. Chop them up and they make the daintiest little cakes for a posh afternoon tea – Lemon & lavender fondant fancies anyone?

And the icing on the cake? They've all been triple-tested in the *Good Food* kitchen, so from the simplest no-bake biscuit slice to herby focaccia made from scratch, you can trust they'll work first time – every time.
Happy baking!

Sarah

Notes and conversion tables

NOTES ON THE RECIPES
• Eggs are large in the UK and Australia and extra large in America unless stated otherwise.
• Wash fresh produce before preparation.
• Recipes contain nutritional analyses for 'sugar', which means the total sugar content including all natural sugars in the ingredients, unless otherwise stated.

APPROXIMATE WEIGHT CONVERSIONS
• All the recipes in this book list both imperial and metric measurements. Conversions are approximate and have been rounded up or down. Follow one set of measurements only; do not mix the two.
• Cup measurements, which are used by cooks in Australia and America, have not been listed here as they vary from ingredient to ingredient. Kitchen scales should be used to measure dry/solid ingredients.

OVEN TEMPERATURES

Gas	°C	°C Fan	°F	Oven temp.
¼	110	90	225	Very cool
½	120	100	250	Very cool
1	140	120	275	Cool or slow
2	150	130	300	Cool or slow
3	160	140	325	Warm
4	180	160	350	Moderate
5	190	170	375	Moderately hot
6	200	180	400	Fairly hot
7	220	200	425	Hot
8	230	210	450	Very hot
9	240	220	475	Very hot

Good Food is concerned about sustainable sourcing and animal welfare. Where possible humanely reared meats, sustainably caught fish (see fishonline. org for further information from the Marine Conservation Society) and free-range chickens and eggs are used when recipes are originally tested.

SPOON MEASURES

Spoon measurements are level unless otherwise specified.

- 1 teaspoon (tsp) = 5ml
- 1 tablespoon (tbsp) = 15ml
- 1 Australian tablespoon = 20ml (cooks in Australia should measure 3 teaspoons where 1 tablespoon is specified in a recipe)

APPROXIMATE LIQUID CONVERSIONS

metric	imperial	AUS	US
50ml	2fl oz	¼ cup	¼ cup
125ml	4fl oz	½ cup	½ cup
175ml	6fl oz	¾ cup	¾ cup
225ml	8fl oz	1 cup	1 cup
300ml	10fl oz/½ pint	½ pint	1¼ cups
450ml	16fl oz	2 cups	2 cups/1 pint
600ml	20fl oz/1 pint	1 pint	2½ cups
1 litre	35fl oz/1¾ pints	1¾ pints	1 quart

Raspberry Bakewell slice

A useful bake to have in your repertoire – this is just as good with a cup of tea as it is served as a traditional, comforting pudding.

TAKES 1 HOUR 20 MINUTES

● **SERVES 10**

375g pack sweet shortcrust pastry
5 tbsp thick seedless raspberry jam
100g/4oz frozen raspberries, just thawed
25g/1oz flaked almonds
4 tbsp apricot jam

FOR THE SPONGE

200g/7oz butter, very soft, plus extra for greasing
200g/7oz golden caster sugar
100g/4oz ground almonds
100g/4oz self-raising flour
1 tsp baking powder
½ tsp almond extract
4 eggs, beaten

1 Heat oven to 200C/180C fan/gas 6. Line the base and sides of a buttered traybake tin, about 18–20cm x 30cm, with baking parchment. Roll out the pastry to line the tin, lift it in and press into the corners. Prick with a fork and chill for 20 minutes.

2 Bake the pastry for 8–10 minutes until it's cooked but not too coloured. Cool for a few minutes and turn down the oven to 180C/160C fan/gas 4.

3 Dot the raspberry jam over the pastry and scatter over the raspberries.

4 For the sponge, put all the ingredients into a large bowl and beat with an electric whisk until soft and very well mixed. Spoon this over the raspberry layer, then smooth evenly. Scatter over the flaked almonds and bake for 35–40 minutes until golden and firm.

5 To serve, warm or cold, melt the apricot jam with 1 tablespoon water and brush over the top of the sponge just before serving.

PER SERVING 595 kcals, protein 9g, carbs 57g, fat 38g, sat fat 16g, fibre 2g, sugar 36g, salt 0.76g

Citrus bars

These bars are essentially a shortbread base with a tangy citrus curd baked on to the top.

TAKES 1 HOUR 5 MINUTES
● MAKES 18 BARS

250g/9oz plain flour
85g/3oz icing sugar, plus extra for dusting
175g/6oz butter, cut into small pieces

FOR THE TOPPING

2 lemons and 1 large orange
4 large eggs
400g/14oz caster sugar
50g/2oz plain flour

1 Heat oven to 180C/160C fan/gas 4. Line the base and sides of a shallow tin, about 23 x 33cm, with baking parchment. Tip the flour, sugar and butter into a food processor and whizz until it forms fine crumbs. Tip into the tin and level with the back of a metal spoon, pressing it down lightly. Bake for 20–25 minutes or until pale golden.

2 To make the topping, finely grate the zest from the lemons and orange, and squeeze out all the juice. Measure the juice – you need 125ml/4½fl oz. Whisk together the eggs and sugar using an electric whisk for 1 minute, then add the citrus zest and juices, and whisk again briefly. Sift in the flour and whisk well. Pour over the shortbread and bake for 15–20 minutes until the topping has set.

3 Cool in the tin, then lift out using the lining paper. Dust with the extra icing sugar and cut into bars.

PER BAR 257 kcals, protein 3g, carbs 39g, fat 10g, sat fat 6g, fibre 1g, sugar 28g, salt 0.2g

Oaty plum–gingerbread slice

This is one of those bakes that will go down well just about any time – at morning coffee or after Sunday lunch with a steaming jug of custard.

TAKES 50 MINUTES

● **CUTS INTO 12 SQUARES**

140g/5oz unsalted butter, plus extra
    for greasing
100g/4oz dark soft brown sugar
100g/4oz golden syrup
6 small plums (about 250g/9oz
    prepared weight)
140g/5oz plain flour
1 tsp baking powder
1 tbsp ground ginger
1 heaped tbsp chopped stem ginger
85g/3oz porridge oats (not jumbo)
2 large eggs, beaten, at room
    temperature

FOR THE TOPPING

25g/1oz plain flour
25g/1oz porridge oats
2 heaped tsp chopped stem ginger

1 Grease a 17 x 23cm cake tin and line with parchment. Heat oven to 180C/160C fan/gas 4. Melt the butter, sugar and syrup together in a large pan. While you wait, stone and quarter the plums.

2 When the pan ingredients are smooth, stir in the flour, baking powder, ¼ teaspoon salt, the gingers, oats and eggs, then beat until well mixed. Pour all but about 2 tablespoons of the batter into the prepared tin, then scatter with the plums.

3 For the topping, mix the flour and oats into the reserved 2 tablespoons of batter to make a flapjack-like dough. Crumble this over the plums and scatter with the chopped ginger. Bake for 30 minutes or until golden and risen, then cool completely in the tin. Cut into squares.

PER SQUARE 248 kcals, protein 4g, carbs 33g, fat 11g, sat fat 6g, fibre 2g, sugar 18g, salt 0.1g

Feelgood flapjacks

These healthier flapjacks use bananas and apple to bind the mixture, so you can cut down on the fat and sugar. But they're still sticky and delicious!

TAKES 1 HOUR 10 MINUTES
● **CUTS INTO 12**

50g/2oz butter, plus extra for greasing
2 tbsp smooth peanut butter
3 tbsp honey or maple syrup
2 ripe bananas, mashed
1 apple, peeled and grated
250g/9oz rolled oats
85g/3oz dried apricots, chopped
100g/4oz raisins
85g/3oz mixed seeds (we used
   pumpkin and sunflower)

1 Heat oven to 160C/140C fan/gas 3. Grease and line a 20cm-square tin with baking parchment. Heat the butter, peanut butter and honey or maple syrup in a small pan until melted. Add the mashed banana, apple and 100ml/3½fl oz hot water, and mix to combine.
2 Tip the oats, the dried fruit and the seeds into a large bowl. Pour in the combined banana and apple, and stir until everything is coated by the wet mixture. Tip into the cake tin and level the surface. Bake for 55 minutes until golden. Leave to cool in the tin. Cut into 12 pieces to serve or store in an airtight container in the fridge. They will keep for up to 3 days.

PER BAR 218 kcals, protein 6g, carbs 29g, fat 8g, sat fat 3g, fibre 4g, sugar 17g, salt 0.1g

Gooseberry & hazelnut slices

A twist on the classic Bakewell flavours of raspberry and almond – this delicious bake pairs fruity, tart gooseberries with crunchy hazelnuts.

TAKES 1¼ HOURS • CUTS INTO 16 SLICES

butter, for greasing
320g/14oz ready-rolled sheet shortcrust pastry
400g/14oz gooseberries
4 tbsp elderflower cordial
25g/1oz cornflour
140g/5oz caster sugar
100g/4oz icing sugar, sifted
50g/2oz toasted hazelnuts, chopped

FOR THE SPONGE
200g/7oz soft butter
200g/7oz caster sugar
100g/4oz ground hazelnuts
100g/4oz self-raising flour
1 tsp baking powder
4 large eggs, beaten

1 Heat oven to 200C/180C fan/gas 6. Grease a deep 20 x 30cm traybake tin. Line with the pastry sheet, then with baking parchment and baking beans. Bake blind for 15 minutes. Remove the paper and beans, and bake for 5 minutes. Reduce oven to 180C/160C fan/gas 4.

2 Put the gooseberries in a pan with 3 tablespoons of the cordial and 3 tablespoons water. Cover and cook for 5 minutes until the berries start to break down. Mix the cornflour and caster sugar, add to the gooseberry mixture then stir until thickened. Spread over the pastry.

3 Put all the sponge ingredients in a large bowl and beat with an electric whisk until smooth. Spread evenly over the gooseberries and bake for 25 minutes until firm to the touch. Cool in the tin.

4 To decorate, mix the icing sugar with the remaining cordial. Drizzle over the cake and scatter over the nuts. Leave until set and cut into fingers.

PER SLICE 413 kcals, protein 5g, carbs 45g, fat 23g, sat fat 9g, fibre 2g, sugar 32g, salt 0.6g

Plum & almond pastry

This pudding looks and tastes fantastic, for very little effort. Serve with custard or ice cream – vanilla or caramel flavours work well.

TAKES 30 MINUTES ● **SERVES 6**

320g all-butter puff pastry sheet
4 tbsp ground almonds
800g/1lb 12oz plums, halved and
    stoned
25g/1oz flaked almonds
3 tbsp caster sugar, plus extra to
    sprinkle

1 Heat oven to 220C/200C fan/gas 7. Line a roughly A4-size traybake tin with baking parchment. Unroll the pastry and line the tin with it. Sprinkle over the ground almonds and then scatter over the plums to make an even layer. Sprinkle with the flaked almonds, then the sugar.

2 Bake for 20 minutes until the pastry is golden and the plums are tender. Allow to stand for 10 minutes to cool a little, then sprinkle with a little more sugar and serve.

PER SERVING 408 kcals, protein 7g, carbs 43g, fat 23g, sat fat 8g, fibre 3g, sugar 23g, salt 0.5g

Apricot shortbread

Adding a fruity layer of apricots elevates a simple shortbread base into a really special bake – perfect for a picnic.

TAKES 45 MINUTES • CUTS INTO 16 SQUARES

250g pack butter, chopped, plus extra for greasing
200g/7oz dried apricots, finely chopped
4 tbsp apricot conserve
100g/4oz golden caster sugar, plus extra for sprinkling
1 tsp vanilla extract
250g/9oz plain flour
140g/5oz ground rice

1 Heat oven to 180C/160C fan/gas 4 and grease and line a 20cm-square shallow cake tin with baking parchment. Put the apricots and conserve in a small pan with 4 tablespoons water, simmer over a medium heat until thick, then mash the apricots with a fork and set aside to cool.
2 Tip the butter, sugar and vanilla into a large bowl, and beat with an electric whisk until pale and fluffy. Add the flour and ground rice, using a wooden spoon and then your hands to bring the mixture together as a dough. Divide into two.
3 Spread one piece of shortbread dough over the bottom of the tin. Spread the apricots over the top, leaving a border around the edge. Roll out the remaining dough to a 20cm square and put on top. Make an indent around the edges of the shortbread, then prick the top with a fork. Bake for 25–30 minutes until the edges start to turn golden. Cool, sprinkle with caster sugar and cut into squares.

PER SQUARE 260 kcals, protein 3g, carbs 32g, fat 13g, sat fat 8g, fibre 2g, sugar 14g, salt 0.3g

Peach Melba roulade

A roulade might look tricky but it's really just a thin traybake, rolled up! This is a great recipe for beginners – simple and foolproof.

TAKES 50 MINUTES, PLUS COOLING
- **CUTS INTO 10 SLICES**

50g/2oz butter, melted, then cooled, plus extra for greasing
6 large eggs
175g/6oz golden caster sugar, plus 3 tbsp for dusting
120g/4½oz self-raising flour, sifted

FOR THE FILLING

1 tsp vanilla extract
420g can peaches in syrup, drained, reserving the syrup, and roughly chopped
200ml/7fl oz double cream
75g/2½oz raspberry coulis
150g pack raspberries

1 Heat oven to 200C/180C fan/gas 6. Butter and line a 25 x 35cm shallow tin with baking parchment. Beat the eggs and sugar using an electric whisk until pale and fluffy – about 5 minutes.
2 Gently fold in the flour using a large metal spoon then fold in the butter. Pour into the tin and smooth to the edges. Bake for 12–15 minutes until springy.
3 Dust a large sheet of parchment with 3 tablespoons sugar. Flip the sponge on to the sugar and peel off the lining parchment. Use the sheet underneath to tightly roll up the sponge then cool.
4 For the filling, whisk the vanilla, 3 tablespoons of peach syrup and cream until soft peaks form. Fold in half of the peaches and ripple in half of the coulis.
5 Unroll the roulade, remove the parchment and spread over the filling. Scatter with the raspberries and remaining peaches, drizzle with the remaining coulis, re-roll and serve.

PER SLICE 345 kcals, protein 6g, carbs 39g, fat 18g, sat fat 10g, fibre 2g, sugar 31g, salt 0.3g

Biscuity lime pie

The perfect addition to an afternoon cup of tea, this zingy citrus slice uses gingernut biscuits for a crunchy base.

TAKES 1 HOUR, PLUS CHILLING
● **CUTS INTO 6 SLICES**

300g pack gingernut biscuits
100g/4oz butter, melted
3 egg yolks
50g/2oz golden caster sugar
zest and juice 4 limes, plus extra thin
   lime slices to decorate (optional)
zest and juice 1 lemon
397g can sweetened condensed milk

1 Heat oven to 180C/160C fan/gas 4. Tip the biscuits into a food processor and blitz to crumbs. Add the butter and pulse to combine. Tip the mixture into a 10 x 34cm fluted rectangular tart tin (or 20cm-round tin) and press into the base and up the sides, right to the edge. Bake for 15 minutes until crisp.
2 Meanwhile, tip the egg yolks, sugar, and lime and lemon zests into a bowl and beat with an electric whisk until doubled in volume. Pour in the condensed milk, beat until combined, then add the citrus juices.
3 Pour the mixture into the tart case and bake for 20 minutes until just set with a slight wobble in the centre. Leave to set completely, then remove from the tin, cool and chill. Top with thin lime slices, if you like and cut into 6 slices to serve.

PER SLICE 633 kcals, protein 10g, carbs 85g, fat 30g, sat fat 15g, fibre 1g, sugar 64g, salt 0.93g

Cinnamon-berry granola bars

Great for lunchboxes, breakfast on the run or just with a cup of coffee. These will keep for up to a week in an airtight tin – if they don't get scoffed first!

TAKES 45 MINUTES • CUTS INTO 12 BARS

100g/4oz butter, plus extra for greasing
200g/7oz porridge oats
100g/4oz sunflower seeds
50g/2oz sesame seeds
50g/2oz chopped walnuts
3 tbsp honey
100g/4oz light muscovado sugar
1 tsp ground cinnamon
100g/4oz dried cranberries, cherries or blueberries, or a mix

1 Heat oven to 160C/140C fan/gas 3. Butter and line the base of an 18 x 25cm tin. Mix the oats, seeds and nuts in a roasting tin, then put in the oven for 5–10 minutes to toast.

2 Meanwhile, warm the butter, honey and sugar in a pan, stirring until the butter is melted. Remove from the heat and add the oat mix, cinnamon and dried fruit, then mix until all the oats are well coated. Tip into the tin, press down lightly, then bake for 30 minutes. Cool in the tin, then cut into 12 bars.

PER BAR 294 kcals, protein 6g, carbs 30g, fat 17g, sat fat 6g, fibre 3g, sugar 17g, salt 0.14g

Apricot & blueberry crumble cake

To peel apricots, make small nicks in their skins with a knife then cover with boiling water for about 40 seconds. The skins should now peel away easily.

TAKES 1 HOUR • CUTS INTO 12 SQUARES

200g/7oz butter, softened
225g/8oz golden caster sugar
225g/8oz self-raising flour
1 tsp baking powder
3 eggs, beaten
2 tbsp milk
150g pot vanilla yogurt
300g/10oz apricots, skinned, halved
    and stoned, or use a drained 410g
    can instead
225g punnet blueberries

FOR THE CRUMBLE

25g/1oz butter, diced
3 heaped tbsp self-raising flour
3 tbsp demerara sugar
1 tsp ground cinnamon

1 Line an oblong traybake tin, about 21 x 30cm, with baking parchment and heat oven to 180C/160C fan/gas 4. Beat the butter, sugar, flour, baking powder, eggs and milk together until creamy. Spoon into the tin, level the top, then bake for 25 minutes until almost set.

2 Meanwhile, get the yogurt and fruit at the ready and make the crumble by rubbing all the ingredients together with your fingers.

3 When the cake has baked for 25 minutes, whip it out of the oven. Working quickly, spoon over the yogurt and scatter over the fruit, then top with the crumble. Return to the oven for 15–20 minutes until a skewer inserted into the cake comes out clean. Serve warm as a pudding, or cooled and cut into 12 squares with tea.

PER SQUARE 443 kcals, protein 8g, carbs 66g, fat 18g, sat fat 11g, fibre 2g, sugar 29g, salt 0.84g

Gooseberry & orange drizzle cake

This cake is simple, fruity and doubles as a pudding if you serve it with custard. If you have more gooseberries in the garden than you can eat, they freeze well in bags.

TAKES 45 MINUTES • CUTS INTO 16–20 SQUARES

225g/8oz softened butter, plus extra for greasing
225g/8oz caster sugar
225g/8oz self-raising flour
4 large eggs
grated zest and juice 1 orange
225g/8oz gooseberries, topped and tailed
140g/5oz granulated sugar

1 Heat oven to 180C/160C fan/gas 4. Butter and line a 20 x 30cm traybake tin with baking parchment.
2 Put the butter, caster sugar, flour, eggs and orange zest in a bowl and beat thoroughly with an electric whisk until creamy and smooth. Stir in the gooseberries, then spoon into the tin and level the surface. Bake for 35 minutes until a skewer inserted into the cake comes out clean.
3 Stir the orange juice and granulated sugar together, spoon over the surface of the warm cake and leave to cool and set. Cut into 16–20 squares.

PER SQUARE (20) 213 kcals, protein 2g, carbs 27g, fat 11g, sat fat 6g, fibre 1g, sugar 20g, salt 0.3g

Gingery plum cake

Choose firm plums so that they keep their shape when cooking. Serve this hearty sponge for afternoon tea or as a pudding with a dollop of something creamy.

TAKES 1 HOUR 25 MINUTES • CUTS INTO 16 SQUARES

butter, for greasing
2 tbsp demerara sugar
500g/1lb 2oz plums

FOR THE CAKE

175g/6oz butter
175g/6oz dark muscovado sugar
140g/5oz golden syrup
2 eggs, beaten
200ml/7fl oz milk
300g/10oz self-raising flour
½ tsp bicarbonate of soda
1 tbsp ground ginger
1 tsp ground mixed spice

1 Heat oven to 180C/160C fan/gas 4. Grease and line the base of a 23cm-square cake tin with baking parchment. Butter the paper generously and sprinkle with the demerara sugar. Halve the plums and arrange in the base of the tin in a single layer, cut-sides down.

2 For the cake, melt the butter, muscovado sugar and syrup in a large pan over a low heat, stirring until smooth. Cool for 10 minutes, then stir in the eggs and milk. Sift in the flour, bicarbonate of soda and spices, then mix to a smooth batter.

3 Pour the batter into the tin, over the plums, and bake for 45–55 minutes until firm to the touch. Cool in the tin for 10 minutes, then turn out on to a wire rack and leave to cool. Will keep in the fridge, wrapped in baking parchment and foil, for up to 5 days.

PER SQUARE 252 kcals, protein 3g, carbs 36g, fat 11g, sat fat 6g, fibre 1g, sugar 24g, salt 0.5g

Raspberry & almond traybake

One mixture – made from ingredients all whizzed in the food processor – makes the base and topping for this super-easy bake.

READY IN 1¼–1½ HOURS • CUTS INTO 16–24 SLICES

250g/9oz self-raising flour
50g/2oz ground almonds
200g/7oz butter, diced
280g/10oz golden granulated sugar
50g/2oz desiccated coconut
2 medium eggs
350–450g/12oz–1lb fresh or frozen raspberries

1 Heat oven to 180C/160C fan/gas 4. Butter a traybake tin about 31 x 17cm. Tip the flour, ground almonds, butter and sugar into a food processor and whizz just until the butter is evenly distributed – or rub together by hand.

2 Remove 85g/3oz of the mix, stir in the coconut and put to one side.

3 Add the eggs to the remaining mixture in the food processor and whizz quickly – or mix with a wooden spoon. It doesn't need to be very smooth. Spread this mixture over the base of the tin, then scatter half the raspberries over the top. Sprinkle with the coconut mixture and bake for 45 minutes.

4 Dot the remaining fruit over the surface. Cook for a further 15 minutes, until firm to the touch. Cool in the tin and cut into 16–24 slices.

PER SLICE (24) 177 kcals, protein 2g, carbs 20g, fat 10g, sat fat 6g, fibre 1g, sugar 13g, salt 0.2g

Tropical fruit traybake

This may look like your standard carrot cake on the outside, but take one bite and you'll realise this fruity bake has hidden depths.

TAKES 1 HOUR • CUTS INTO 15 SQUARES

175ml/6fl oz vegetable oil, plus extra for greasing
175g/6oz dark muscovado sugar
3 large eggs
1 small ripe banana, mashed
140g/5oz grated eating apples
100g/4oz grated carrots
1 small mango, peeled and cut into small dice
zest 1 lemon
250g/9oz self-raising flour
1 tsp bicarbonate of soda
1 tsp ground mixed spice

FOR THE ICING

225g/8oz icing sugar, sieved
75g/2½oz passion fruit or lemon curd
75g/2½oz cream cheese

1 Heat oven to 180C/160C fan/gas 4. Grease and line a 22cm-square tin with baking parchment. Whisk the oil and sugar in a large mixing bowl until light and fluffy. Beat in the eggs, one at a time, followed by the banana. Stir through the apples, carrots, mango and lemon zest. Combine the flour, bicarb and mixed spice in another bowl, then fold into the fruit mixture.

2 Pour the mixture into the tin and bake for 40 minutes, until a skewer inserted into the cake comes out clean. Cool for 10 minutes before turning out on to a wire rack.

3 To make the icing, beat together the icing sugar, passion fruit or lemon curd and the cream cheese. Spread over the top of the cake and cut into squares to serve.

PER SQUARE 339 kcals, protein 3g, carbs 45g, fat 16g, sat fat 4g, fibre 2g, sugar 33g, salt 0.4g

Nutty plum-crumble slice

Like plum crumble? Then you'll love this. If you don't have a food processor, rub the ingredients for step 1 together with your fingers, then use an electric whisk.

TAKES 1 HOUR 20 MINUTES • CUTS INTO 16 SLICES

250g pack butter (this must be very cold), plus extra for greasing

225g/8oz caster sugar, plus extra for sprinkling

300g/10oz ground almonds

140g/5oz plain flour, plus extra 25g/1oz for the filling

2 eggs

1 tsp ground cinnamon, plus extra for sprinkling

1 tsp baking powder

about 6 plums, stoned and each cut into six

50g/2oz flaked almonds

1 Heat oven to 180C/160C fan/gas 4. Butter and line a 20 x 30cm traybake tin with baking paper. Pulse the butter, sugar and ground almonds in a food processor, until it resembles rough breadcrumbs. Set aside half the mix in a bowl.

2 Add 140g/5oz flour to the processor and whizz until it forms a dough. Tip into the tin and press down with the back of a spoon. Bake for 15–20 minutes until golden. Leave to cool for 10 minutes.

3 To make the filling, put the remaining butter, sugar and almond mix back into the processor, reserving 3 tablespoons for the topping. Add the eggs, the 25g/1oz flour, cinnamon and baking powder, and whizz to a soft batter. Spread over the base.

4 Top with the plum pieces and a little caster sugar and cinnamon. Bake for 20 minutes, then sprinkle with the reserved crumble mix and the flaked almonds. Cook for another 20 minutes or until golden. Leave to cool in the tin.

PER SLICE 360 kcals, protein 7g, carbs 26g, fat 26g, sat fat 9g, fibre 2g, sugar 18g, salt 0.37g

Leftover veg & orange cake

This is a brilliant way to use up leftover vegetables that are on their way out – don't think you have to stick to one type either, a mixture adds depth of flavour.

TAKES 1 HOUR 10 MINUTES ● CUTS INTO 15 SQUARES

200g/7oz butter, melted, plus extra for greasing
140g/5oz sultanas or raisins
zest and juice 2 oranges or 4 clementines
300g/10oz self-raising flour
300g/10oz light soft brown sugar
2 tsp ground mixed spice
1 tsp ground ginger
1 tsp bicarbonate of soda
4 large eggs, beaten with a fork
300g/10oz carrots, parsnips, pumpkin, butternut squash or swede, or a mixture, grated
200g/7oz icing sugar
few crushed white sugar cubes

1 Heat oven to 180C/160C fan/gas 4. Grease and line a 30 x 20cm traybake tin with baking parchment. Mix the sultanas or raisins and zest and juice from 1 orange, or 2 clementines, and microwave on High for 2 minutes.

2 Mix the flour, brown sugar, spices, bicarb and a pinch of salt in a large bowl. Mix the eggs with the melted butter and the sultana or raisin mixture, then tip that into the dry ingredients and mix. Stir in the grated veg and scrape into the tin. Bake for 35–40 minutes, or until a skewer poked in the centre comes out clean. Cool in the tin.

3 Once cool, sift the icing sugar into a bowl and stir in the remaining orange or clementine zest plus enough of the juice to make a runny icing. Drizzle all over the cake and scatter with the crushed sugar cubes. Leave to set, then slice into 15 squares to serve.

PER SQUARE 346 kcals, protein 4g, carbs 55g, fat 13g, sat fat 7g, fibre 1g, sugar 40g, salt 0.7g

Coconut & mango sponge

Yummy tinned mango and crunchy coconut all baked in one sponge – this is as tasty as it is cheap to make, and good served with an extra dollop of coconut yogurt.

TAKES 1 HOUR • CUTS INTO 15 SQUARES

200g/7oz butter, softened, plus extra
    for greasing
425g can sliced mango in syrup,
    drained
225g/8oz golden caster sugar
4 large eggs
200g/7oz self-raising flour
50g/2oz desiccated coconut
140g/5oz Greek style coconut yogurt

1 Heat oven to 180C/160C fan/gas 4. Grease and line a 20 x 30cm traybake tin with two strips of baking parchment. Dry the mango slices on some kitchen paper, then chop into 3cm pieces and set aside.
2 Beat the butter and sugar together until creamy. Beat in the eggs, one at a time, then use a spatula to fold through the flour and coconut, followed by the yogurt and mango. Scrape the mixture into the tin and scatter over a little more coconut. Bake for 30 minutes until risen and golden, and a skewer inserted into the centre of the cake comes out clean. Leave to cool.

PER SQUARE 231 kcals, protein 4g, carbs 28g, fat 12g, sat fat 7g, fibre 2g, sugar 18g, salt 0.3g

Fudgy coconut brownies

*These gorgeous little brownies don't have the gooey centre of some, but their dense,
fudgy quality will have you reaching for a second in no time.*

**TAKES 1 HOUR • CUTS INTO
16 SQUARES**

100g/4oz cocoa powder
250g/9oz butter
500g/1lb 2oz golden caster sugar
4 large eggs, beaten
100g/4oz self-raising flour
100g/4oz desiccated coconut
icing sugar, to dust (optional)

1 Heat oven to 180C/160C fan/gas 4.
Line the base of a 21cm-square tin with
baking parchment. Put the cocoa, butter
and sugar in your largest pan and gently
melt, stirring so the mixture doesn't
catch. When the cocoa mixture is melted
and combined, cool slightly, then stir in
the eggs, little by little, followed by the
flour and coconut.
2 Tip into the tin and bake for 45 minutes
on a middle shelf – check the brownies
after 30 minutes and cover with another
piece of baking parchment if the crust is
browning too much. Cool in the tin, then
carefully lift out, dust with icing sugar, if
you like, and cut into squares.

PER SQUARE 358 kcals, protein 3g, carbs 43g,
fat 21g, sat fat 13g, fibre 2g, sugar 35g,
salt 0.39g

Better beetroot brownies

Nutritious beetroot adds sweetness, and its juiciness means you can reduce the amount of fat used. Swapping butter for rapeseed oil here makes this treat dairy free!

TAKES 1 HOUR • **CUTS INTO 12 SQUARES**

500g/1lb 2oz cooked beetroots (not in vinegar), peeled
100ml/3½fl oz rapeseed oil
3 large eggs
200g/7oz golden caster sugar
2 tsp vanilla extract
250g/9oz good-quality dark chocolate (70% cocoa, dairy-free if you want), melted
140g/5oz plain flour
75g/2½oz cocoa powder
1 tsp baking powder
50g/2oz walnut pieces, roughly chopped
100g/4oz icing sugar

1 Heat oven to 180C/160C fan/gas 4. Grease and line a 20 x 30cm traybake tin with baking parchment. Chop one-third of the beetroots into small cubes and set aside. Blitz the remainder to a paste in a blender or food processor. Sit the paste in a sieve over a bowl and collect 1–2 tablespoons juice. Save this for the icing, and mix the oil into the purée.
2 Use an electric whisk to beat the eggs, sugar and vanilla together in a large mixing bowl until light, fluffy and tripled in size. Carefully fold this into the beetroot mixture with the melted chocolate. Fold in the flour, cocoa powder and baking powder, then the walnuts and chopped beetroot.
3 Pour the mixture into the tin and bake for 20–25 minutes until slightly gooey in the middle. Cool. Mix enough reserved beetroot juice with the icing sugar to get a runny icing. Remove the brownies from the tin, drizzle with the icing and slice.

PER SQUARE 408 kcals, protein 7g, carbs 50g, fat 20g, sat fat 6g, fibre 3g, sugar 41g, salt 0.4g

Best-ever chocolate–raspberry brownies

No baking book would be complete without this, our best brownie recipe ever. You can swap the raspberries for other berries if you like.

TAKES 50 MINUTES • CUTS INTO 15 SQUARES

200g/7oz dark chocolate, broken into chunks

100g/4oz milk chocolate, broken into chunks

250g pack salted butter

400g/14oz light soft brown sugar

4 large eggs

140g/5oz plain flour

50g/2oz cocoa powder

200g/7oz raspberries

1 Heat oven to 180C/160C fan/gas 4. Line a 20 x 30cm traybake tin with baking parchment. Put the chocolates, butter and sugar in a pan and gently melt, stirring occasionally with a wooden spoon. Remove from the heat.

2 Stir the eggs, one by one, into the melted chocolate mixture. Sift over the flour and cocoa, and stir in. Stir in half the raspberries, scrape into the tin, then scatter over the remaining raspberries. Bake on the middle shelf for 30 minutes or, if you prefer a firmer texture, for 5 minutes more.

3 Cool before slicing into 15 squares. Store in an airtight container for up to 3 days.

PER SQUARE 389 kcals, protein 5g, carbs 44g, fat 22g, sat fat 13g, fibre 2g, sugar 38g, salt 0.4g

Gluten-free fudgy chocolate squares

Deeply chocolatey – if you're feeling really decadent, serve these as a dessert with ice cream. Your kids will love them, and you'd never guess they were gluten free.

TAKES 1 HOUR 5 MINUTES • CUTS INTO 16 SQUARES

FOR THE CAKE

200g/7oz butter, chopped

200g/7oz gluten-free dark chocolate, roughly chopped

350g/12oz golden caster sugar

50g/2oz gluten-free self-raising flour

50g/2oz cocoa powder

50g/2oz ground almonds

1 tsp xanthan gum

4 large eggs, beaten

50g/2oz walnuts, broken or roughly chopped

FOR THE ICING AND DECORATION

100g/4oz butter, chopped

2 heaped tbsp cocoa powder

200g/7oz icing sugar, sifted

2 tbsp milk

50g/2oz walnuts, broken or roughly chopped, to scatter

1 Heat oven to 180C/160C fan/gas 4 and line a 20 x 30cm traybake tin with baking parchment. Tip the butter and chocolate into a non-stick pan and melt over a low heat. Stir occasionally, until smooth – do not overheat. Leave to cool.

2 Meanwhile, mix the sugar, flour, cocoa and almonds with the xanthan gum. Stir into the chocolate mixture, then beat in the eggs and walnuts. Scrape into the tin and bake for 30–35 minutes until firm and just cooked – when tested with a skewer, the crumb should still be a little moist. Cool in the tin.

3 To make the icing, melt the butter in a non-stick pan. Stir in the cocoa and cook, stirring, for about 1 minute. Add the icing sugar and milk, and beat well. Pour on top of the cooled cake, scatter with the walnuts and lightly press them in. Leave until set then remove from the tin, strip off the baking parchment and cut into 16 squares.

PER SQUARE 448 kcals, protein 5g, carbs 45g, fat 28g, sat fat 14g, fibre 2g, sugar 42g, salt 0.5g

Chocolate, raspberry & rose tart

This chilled traybake is a little bit special – perfect for entertaining when you want to impress, but with no last-minute stress.

TAKES 35 MINUTES, PLUS AT LEAST 5 HOURS CHILLING • CUTS INTO 15 SQUARES

200g/7oz bourbon biscuits
85g/3oz crunchy amaretti biscuits
140g/5oz salted butter, melted, plus extra for greasing
75g/2½oz golden caster sugar
a few cubes best-quality Turkish delight, diced, to decorate

FOR THE FILLING

400ml/14fl oz double cream
200g/7oz dark chocolate, broken into chunks
200g/7oz milk chocolate, broken into chunks
140g/5oz raspberries, plus a handful more to decorate

FOR THE ROSE CRÈME FRAÎCHE

400g/14oz crème fraîche
2 tbsp icing sugar, sifted
2 tsp rosewater

1 Double-bag the bourbon biscuits in food bags and bash to crumbs with a rolling pin. Repeat with the amaretti biscuits. Stir into the melted butter with the sugar. Grease and line the base and sides of an 18 x 28cm loose-bottomed tin with baking parchment. Press the biscuit mixture into the base and chill for 30 minutes.

2 Put the cream for the filling and all the chocolate chunks in a heatproof bowl over a pan of barely simmering water. Gently melt, stirring very occasionally.

3 Dot the raspberries over the biscuit base, pour over the chocolate and chill for at least 5 hours until firm.

4 To serve, remove from the fridge and, after 15 minutes, lift from tin then peel off the parchment. Scatter with a few more raspberries and the diced Turkish delight. Mix the crème fraîche, icing sugar and rosewater. Cut the tart into 15 squares and serve with the rose crème fraîche.

PER SQUARE 572 kcals, protein 5g, carbs 38g, fat 45g, sat fat 28g, fibre 2g, sugar 33g, salt 0.3g

Chocolate–orange squares

This flavour combination is a match made in heaven – and it's really worth seeking out a good-flavoured orange chocolate for the hidden chunks.

TAKES 1 HOUR 5 MINUTES • CUTS INTO 12–18 SQUARES

200g/7oz butter, chopped
200g/7oz dark chocolate, roughly chopped
zest 1 large orange
4 large eggs
350g/12oz caster sugar
100g/4oz plain flour
50g/2oz cocoa powder
100g/4oz dark chocolate with orange, chopped into small chunks

1 Heat oven to 180C/160C fan/gas 4 and line a 24 x 20cm traybake tin with baking parchment. Put the butter, dark chocolate and orange zest in a non-stick pan and very gently melt over a low heat, stirring every now and then, until smooth – take care not to overheat the mix. Leave to cool.

2 Whisk the eggs and sugar together with an electric whisk until the mixture is pale, has doubled in volume and leaves a trail when the beaters are lifted. Gently stir into the cooled chocolate mixture. Sift over the flour and cocoa, stir in, then add the orange-chocolate chunks.

3 Pour into the lined tin and bake for 35–40 minutes. Cool in the tin, then cut into 12–18 squares.

PER SQUARE (18) 291 kcals, protein 3g, carbs 33g, fat 16g, sat fat 9g, fibre 1g, sugar 29g, salt 0.3g

Nutty chocolate crunch

Little chocolatey bites studded with nuts and dried fruit. Make them then package them up as a gift – they're lovely with coffee.

TAKES 25 MINUTES, PLUS CHILLING

● **CUTS INTO 20 SQUARES**

100g/4oz butter, chopped, plus extra for greasing

250g/9oz assorted biscuits, roughly chopped

250g/9oz assorted nuts or a mix of nuts and dried fruit

300g/10oz milk or dark chocolate, or a mixture of both, chopped

140g/5oz golden syrup

1 Butter and line a 20cm-square cake tin with non-stick baking parchment. In a large bowl, combine the biscuits and nuts or mix of nuts and dried fruit, halving any larger nuts. Melt the chocolate, butter and golden syrup in a bowl set over a pan of simmering water, stirring occasionally, until smooth and glossy, then pour this over the biscuit and nut/nut and dried fruit mixture.

2 Tip the mixture into the tin, then flatten lightly – it doesn't need to be completely smooth. Chill for at least 2 hours or overnight before cutting into 20 squares.

PER SQUARE 267 kcals, protein 5g, carbs 24g, fat 18g, sat fat 7g, fibre 1g, sugar 18g, salt 0.27g

Chocolate & pecan traybake

Another gluten-free bake to please the whole family, but if you don't have a gluten allergy, just use normal breadcrumbs instead.

TAKES 40 MINUTES • CUTS INTO 12 SQUARES

200g/7oz dark chocolate, chopped
100g/4oz unsalted butter
85g/3oz caster sugar
4 eggs, separated
85g/3oz ground almonds
5 tbsp fresh gluten-free breadcrumbs
140g/5oz pecan nut halves

1 Heat oven to 180C/160C fan/gas 4. Line a 25cm-square cake tin with non-stick baking parchment. Put the chocolate and butter in a large microwave-proof bowl, cover and cook on High for 30 seconds. Stir, then continue to cook for 30 seconds more, or until the chocolate has nearly melted. When cooled slightly, but still melted, stir in half the sugar and all the egg yolks.

2 Whisk the egg whites to stiff peaks. Add the remaining sugar and whisk again until glossy and thick. Stir in 1 tablespoon to the chocolate mixture to loosen, along with the ground almonds and breadcrumbs, then fold through the rest gently. Transfer to the tin and top with pecans. Bake for 25–30 minutes. Cool in the tin for 10 minutes, then lift on to a wire rack to cool completely. Cut into 12 squares to serve.

PER SQUARE 347 kcals, protein 6g, carbs 25g, fat 26g, sat fat 9g, fibre 2g, sugar 20g, salt 0.2g

Cherry–oat squares with chocolate drizzle

These oaty squares can be made in minutes using ingredients you probably already have in your cupboard.

TAKES 45 MINUTES • CUTS INTO 16 SQUARES

140g/5oz butter, melted, plus extra
    for greasing
100g/4oz self-raising flour
175g/6oz caster sugar
175g/6oz porridge oats
1 egg, beaten
100g/4oz glacé cherries, halved
50g/2oz dark chocolate

1 Heat oven to 180C/160C fan/gas 4. Butter and line the base and sides of a 22cm-square cake tin: cut two strips of baking parchment the width of the tin and longer than the base and sides, and fit into the tin each way and up the sides. This will make lifting the cake out easier.

2 Mix together the flour, sugar and oats in a bowl. Add the egg, melted butter and cherries, and mix well. Tip into the tin and spread evenly with a fork.

3 Bake for 20–25 minutes until golden brown. Cool in the tin for 10 minutes, then carefully lift out using the paper and put on a board. Mark, but don't cut, four lines each way to make sixteen squares.

4 Melt the dark chocolate in the microwave for 1 minute, then drizzle it over the squares. When the chocolate has set, cut into squares down the marked lines.

PER SQUARE 208 kcals, protein 3g, carbs 27g, fat 9g, sat fat 5g, fibre 2g, sugar 17g, salt 0.2g

Apricot, raspberry & white-chocolate buckle

Apricots and raspberries are really good partners, and are especially good baked into this soft vanilla cake topped with cinnamon crumble.

TAKES 1¼ HOURS • SERVES 8

175g/6oz self-raising flour, plus
   2 rounded tbsp
2 tbsp demerara sugar
2 tsp ground cinnamon
175g/6oz caster sugar
3 eggs
2 tsp vanilla extract
6 apricots, stoned and sliced
200g/7oz raspberries, fresh or frozen
200g/7oz white chocolate chips or
   chunks

1 Heat oven to 180C/160C fan/gas 4. Line the base of a 23cm square tin. For the crumble mix, put 2 tablespoons flour and 25g/1oz of the butter with the demerara sugar and cinnamon in a bowl. Rub between your fingers until it resembles damp breadcrumbs.
2 Tip the remaining flour and butter and the caster sugar, eggs and vanilla in a bowl, then beat until well combined. Lightly fold in half of the apricots, raspberries and chocolate chips or chunks. Spread into the prepared tin.
3 Scatter over the remaining fruit and chocolate, then sprinkle with the crumble mix. Bake for 45–50 minutes until light golden. Cool for 10 minutes and remove from the tin. Cut into squares and serve warm with cream or ice cream for dessert, or cold for tea.

PER SERVING 437 kcals, protein 6g, carbs 53g, fat 24g, sat fat 14g, fibre 2g, sugar 33g, salt 0.72g

Marbled chocolate brownies

Marry rich, dark brownie with a creamy white chocolate 'blondie' and you've got a great bake for the biscuit tin or a decadent pud to serve warm with vanilla ice cream.

TAKES 1 HOUR 10 MINUTES
- **CUTS INTO 16 SQUARES**

200g/7oz dark chocolate (at least 70% cocoa)
200g/7oz white chocolate
250g pack unsalted butter, cut into cubes
300g/10oz golden caster sugar
4 eggs, beaten
140g/5oz plain flour

1 Butter and line a 23cm-square brownie tin and heat oven to 180C/160C fan/gas 4. Put the dark and white chocolates into two separate large bowls and add half of the butter to each. One bowl at a time, heat in the microwave on Low for 1½ minutes, stirring halfway, until melted.

2 Add half of the sugar and 2 of the beaten eggs to each bowl, then beat until smooth. Now stir 50g/2oz of the flour into the dark-chocolate mix and the remaining flour into the white mix.

3 Spoon tablespoons of the batter into the tin, alternating dark and white. Once the bottom of the tin is covered, go over the first layer, spooning white on top of the dark blobs and dark on top of the white. To marble the brownies, pull a skewer through the tin several times.

4 Bake for 35 minutes or until the middle of the brownie is just set and the white-chocolate patches on top have a pale golden crust. Leave to cool.

PER SQUARE 379 kcals, protein 5g, carbs 40g, fat 24g, sat fat 14g, fibre 1g, sugar 31g, salt 0.09g

Chocolate & caramel flapjacks

Flapjacks are best made in advance, the base will be stickier and toppings firmer, so they're the perfect bake to fill the tin with before a camping holiday.

TAKES 1 HOUR 10 MINUTES • CUTS INTO 12 MINI SQUARES

200g/7oz soft brown sugar
200g/7oz butter, plus extra for greasing
2 tbsp golden syrup
350g/12oz whole oats
397g can caramel
200g/7oz plain chocolate
1 tbsp unflavoured oil, like sunflower

1 Heat oven to 150C/130C fan/gas 2. Place the sugar, butter and golden syrup together in a saucepan and gently heat until the butter has melted, stirring occasionally. Take the saucepan off the heat and stir in the oats, mixing thoroughly. Pour the mixture into a lined and lightly greased 22cm square tin, pressing it out evenly using the back of a wooden spoon. Bake in the centre of the oven for 40–45 minutes.

2 Allow the mixture to cool in the tin for 10 minutes (or for best results, leave to cool completely overnight), then evenly spread over the caramel. Chill until firm.

3 Melt the chocolate in a heatproof bowl set over a pan of barely simmering water, then stir in the oil and pour the mixture over the chilled caramel flapjack base. Let the chocolate set, then cut into squares.

PER SQUARE 492 kcals, protein 8g, carbs 67g, fat 23g, sat fat 13g, fibre 4g, sugar 48g, salt 0.37g

Mini chocolate & ginger bites

A sticky chocolate traybake dotted with crystallised ginger then cut into little chunks makes for the perfect sweet canapé.

TAKES 1 HOUR ● CUTS INTO 36 SQUARES

150g bar dark chocolate, broken into chunks
250g pack salted butter
200g/7oz soft brown sugar
140g/5oz self-raising flour
50g/2oz cocoa powder, sifted
3 large eggs, beaten
120g/4½oz crystallised ginger, chopped
icing sugar, to dust

1 Heat oven to 180C/160C fan/gas 4 and line a 20cm-square cake tin with baking parchment. Melt the dark chocolate with the butter in the microwave or in a heatproof bowl over just simmering water.
2 Mix together the sugar, flour and cocoa powder, and stir in the melted chocolate and butter mixture, then the eggs. Stir through the crystallised ginger.
3 Pour into the tin and smooth the surface. Bake for 35–40 minutes. Allow to cool thoroughly before slicing into 36 small bites. Arrange on a platter and sprinkle with icing sugar before serving.

PER SQUARE 132 kcals, protein 2g, carbs 13g, fat 8g, sat fat 5g, fibre 1g, sugar 9g, salt 0.2g

Chocolate, cranberry & macadamia squares

It's worth using macadamias for this recipe because they're 'crisper' than other nuts; their texture works wonderfully with the buttery sponge.

TAKES 40 MINUTES • CUTS INTO 12 SQUARES

150g bar dark chocolate, broken into chunks
200g/7oz butter
200g/7oz soft brown sugar
140g/5oz self-raising flour, sifted
50g/2oz cocoa powder, sifted
3 large eggs, beaten
50g/2oz dried cranberries
100g/4oz macadamia nuts
50g/2oz cranberry sauce

1 Heat oven to 180C/160C fan/gas 4 and line a 20cm-square baking tin with baking parchment. Melt the dark chocolate with the butter in the microwave or in a heatproof bowl over just simmering water.

2 Mix together the sugar, flour and cocoa powder and stir in the melted chocolate and butter mixture, followed by the eggs. Stir through the dried cranberries and macadamia nuts, then swirl through the cranberry sauce.

3 Pour into the tin and smooth the surface. Bake for 25–30 minutes. Allow to cool before slicing into 12 squares.

PER SQUARE 399 kcals, protein 5g, carbs 38g, fat 26g, sat fat 13g, fibre 1.8g, sugar 29g, salt 0.5g

Chocolate flapjacks

Lovely for a lunchtime treat, these flapjacks have plenty of slow-burning carbs to keep you going through the afternoon.

TAKES 45 MINUTES • CUTS INTO 8 BARS

50g/2oz butter
50g/2oz clear honey
350g/12oz granola (or make your own with our recipe below)
100g/4oz dark chocolate, half chopped into small chunks, half melted

HOMEMADE GRANOLA

100g/4oz honey
2 tbsp sunflower oil
150g/5oz rolled oats
50g/2oz whole almonds (with skins)
½ tsp ground cinnamon
70g/3oz dried apricots, roughly chopped

1 If you're making your own granola, heat oven on to 180C/160C fan/gas 4. Melt the honey and oil together, then stir in the oats, almonds and cinnamon to coat. Spread on large baking sheets and cook for 20–25 minutes until golden – then stir in the apricots.

2 To make the flapjacks, turn the oven up to 190C/170C fan/gas 5 and line an 18cm-square (or 15 x 20cm) cake tin with baking parchment. Melt the butter and honey together in a large pan.

3 Stir in the granola and the chocolate chunks with a wooden spoon, making sure they are all well coated.

4 Tip the flapjack mix into the tin and press down very firmly (a potato masher is a good tool to use here). Cover with foil or more baking parchment, then bake for 25–30 minutes. Leave to cool in the tin, then drizzle over the melted chocolate. Once set, cut into eight portions. Can be stored in an airtight container for 3 days.

PER BAR 315 kcals, protein 5g, carbs 39g, fat 17g, sat fat 6g, fibre 3g, sugar 27g, salt 0.12g

Chocolate gingerbread bars with ginger-fudge icing

These bars are based on a classic flourless-chocolate-cake style, so they're rich but light in equal measure.

TAKES 1 HOUR ● CUTS INTO 15 BARS

250g/9oz butter, plus extra for greasing
400g/14oz dark chocolate, broken
    into chunks
25g/1oz cocoa powder
250g/9oz golden caster sugar
1 tbsp ground ginger
140g/5oz ground almonds
6 large eggs, separated

FOR THE ICING

100g/4oz butter, cubed
50g/2oz dark chocolate (use a bar,
    broken into pieces, or chips)
50g/2oz cocoa powder
200g/7oz icing sugar, sifted
2 tbsp ground ginger
few chunks crystallised ginger, diced

1 Heat oven to 180C/160C fan/gas 4. Grease a 20 x 30cm baking tin and line the base and sides with baking parchment. Melt the chocolate, cocoa, sugar and butter together in a pan over a very low heat. Once melted, remove from the heat and stir in the ginger and almonds, followed by the egg yolks, one at a time.

2 In a clean bowl, beat the egg whites until stiff, then stir a couple of spoonfuls into the chocolate mixture. Very gently fold in the rest with a metal spoon.

3 Gently scrape the mixture into the tin. Bake for 30–35 minutes. Sit the cake tin on a wire rack and cool.

4 Put the butter, chocolate, cocoa, icing sugar, ground ginger and 4 tablespoons water in a pan. Heat gently, stirring, until smooth. Pour over the cake, leave for 1–2 minutes to cool slightly, then scatter over the ginger. Cool until set.

PER BAR 553 kcals, protein 7g, carbs 51g, fat 36g, sat fat 19g, fibre 2g, sugar 49g, salt 0.6g

Crispy chocolate fridge cake

This recipe is a great option for first-time cooks, as the traybake is set in the fridge; so there's no need to use an oven.

TAKES 20 MINUTES, PLUS CHILLING
- **CUTS INTO 16–20 CHUNKS**

300g/10oz dark chocolate
100g/4oz butter, diced
140g/5oz golden syrup
1 tsp vanilla extract
200g/7oz biscuits, roughly chopped
100g/4oz sultanas
85g/3oz Rice Krispies
100–140g/4–5oz mini eggs (optional)
50g/2oz white chocolate, melted

1 Cover the bottom of a 20 x 30cm cake tin with a sheet of baking parchment. Break the chocolate into chunks and put them in a big glass bowl. Put the butter and golden syrup into the bowl too.

2 Sit the bowl over a pan of just simmering water (grown-ups can do this bit). Melt the chocolate, butter and golden syrup together, stirring occasionally with a wooden spoon, until smooth and glossy.

3 Lift the bowl away from the pan (grown ups may need to help). Tip in the vanilla, biscuits, sultanas and Rice Krispies, and mix until everything is coated.

4 Tip all the mixture into the tin, then flatten it down with the back of your wooden spoon. Press in some mini eggs, if using, and put the cake in the fridge until set.

5 When the fridge cake is hard, drizzle the top with melted white chocolate. Set in the fridge before cutting into chunks.

PER CHUNK (20) 249 kcals, protein 2g, carbs 32g, fat 12g, sat fat 7g, fibre 1g, sugar 24g, salt 0.4g

Raspberry & apple crumble slices

The best bits of two great puds – buttery crumble and super-light sponge – combined in one tasty treat.

TAKES 1 HOUR 5 MINUTES • CUTS INTO 16 SLICES

1 Bramley apple, peeled and diced
100g/4oz butter, softened
175g/6oz golden caster sugar
1 large egg
280g/10oz self-raising flour
125ml/4fl oz milk
200g/7oz raspberries

FOR THE CRUMBLE TOPPING

50g/2oz butter, diced
85g/3oz self-raising flour
100g/4oz golden caster sugar
zest 1 lemon

1 Heat oven to 180C/160C fan/gas 4 and line a 20 x 30cm cake tin with baking parchment. Put the apple in a small pan with 2 tablespoons water. Cook for a few minutes, until the apple starts to soften.

2 Meanwhile, make the crumble topping. Rub the butter into the flour, sugar and lemon zest until it resembles big breadcrumbs, then set aside.

3 Beat the butter and sugar in a large bowl until fluffy, then gradually add the egg. Tip in the flour and milk, and continue to beat until everything is combined. Spoon the mixture into the tin, smooth the surface, then dot with the raspberries. Sprinkle over the crumble topping and ask a grown-up to bake for 45 minutes or until a skewer inserted into the centre comes out clean, and the topping is golden.

PER SLICE 230 kcals, protein 3g, carbs 37g, fat 9g, sat fat 5g, fibre 1g, sugar 21g, salt 0.35g

Yummy chocolate log

Kids will love making, decorating and munching on this yummy chocolate log.

TAKES 40 MINUTES, PLUS COOLING

- **SERVES 8**

butter, for greasing

3 eggs

85g/3oz golden caster sugar

85g/3oz plain flour

2 tbsp cocoa powder

½ tsp baking powder

FOR THE FILLING & ICING

50g/2oz butter

140g/5oz dark chocolate, broken into
   squares

1 tbsp golden syrup

284ml pot double cream

200g/7oz icing sugar, plus extra to dust

2–3 extra-strong mints, crushed

holly sprigs, to decorate (remove the
   berries before serving)

1 Heat oven to 200C/180C fan/gas 6.
Grease and line a 23 x 32cm cake tin with
baking parchment. Beat the eggs and
sugar with an electric whisk until thick .

2 Mix the flour, cocoa and baking
powder, then sift on to the egg mixture.
Fold in carefully with a big metal spoon.
Pour into the tin and bake for 10 minutes.

3 Tip the cake on to a sheet of baking
parchment. Peel off the paper stuck to
the cake. Roll up the cake from a long
edge with the fresh paper inside. Cool.

4 Get a grown-up to melt the butter and
chocolate together. Stir in the syrup and
5 tablespoons of the cream. Stir in the
icing sugar until smooth. Whisk the
remaining cream until thick. Unroll the
cake and spread with the cream, scatter
the mints, then roll up again into a log.

5 Cut a diagonal slice from one end and
stick back on to the cake at an angle.
Spread the icing. Use a fork to mark it like
bark. Decorate with icing sugar and holly.

PER SERVING 552 kcals, protein 5g, carbs 64g,
fat 32g, sat fat 18g, fibre 1g, sugar 54g, salt 0.3g

Frosted carrot squares

A homemade carrot cake is a great way to get children to eat more vegetables! You can also try swapping carrots for sweet potatoes or butternut squash.

TAKES 1 HOUR, PLUS COOLING
● **CUTS INTO 6–12 SQUARES**
200g/7oz carrots, peeled
175g/6oz soft brown sugar
200g/7oz self-raising flour
1 tsp bicarbonate of soda
2 tsp ground cinnamon
zest 1 orange
2 eggs
150ml/¼ pint sunflower oil

FOR THE ICING
50g/2oz soft butter
75g/2½oz icing sugar
200g/7oz cream cheese
your favourite sprinkles (optional)

1 Heat oven to 180C/160C fan/gas 4. Line an 18cm-square cake tin with baking parchment. Grate the carrots on the fine side of a grater, then tip them into a large bowl. Tip the sugar, flour, bicarb and cinnamon on top of the carrot, then add the orange zest and mix everything around a bit.

2 Break the eggs into a bowl, then add them to the bowl along with the oil. Mix everything together well. Scrape the cake mix into the tin and level the top. Ask a grown-up to put it in the oven for 30 minutes or until the cake is cooked. Leave to cool.

3 Make the icing: mix the butter and icing sugar together, then stir in the cream cheese until smooth. When the cake is cool, spread the top with the icing and cut into 6–12 squares. Decorate with sprinkles, if you like.

PER SQUARE (6) 665 kcals, protein 8g, carbs 72g, fat 40g, sat fat 13g, fibre 2g, sugar 47g, salt 1.33g

Treacle tart bars

Everybody loves treacle tart, and everybody loves flapjacks, so we think this clever combination is going to be popular!

TAKES 1 HOUR 20 MINUTES • CUTS INTO 16 BARS

1 sheet ready-rolled shortcrust pastry
750g/1lb 10oz golden syrup
175g/6oz soft breadcrumbs
120g/4½oz rolled oats
zest and juice 1 lemon
3 large eggs, beaten with a fork

1 Heat oven to 200C/180C fan/gas 6. Line the base and sides of a 20 x 30cm tin with baking parchment (2 lengths criss-crossing is the easiest way). Unroll the pastry and use it to line the base of the tin. Lay a sheet of baking parchment on top, add some baking beans and bake for 20 minutes. Remove the beans and paper then bake for 10 more minutes. Lower the oven temperature to 180C/160C fan/gas 4.

2 Mix together the golden syrup, breadcrumbs, oats, lemon zest and juice and the eggs. Tip this mixture over the pastry, spread evenly, then bake for 40 minutes until the filling is golden brown and feels set to the touch. Cool, then slice into bars.

PER BAR 282 kcals, protein 5g, carbs 54g, fat 6g, sat fat 2g, fibre 2g, sugar 36g, salt 0.7g

Mint-chocolate tree cake

Kids love Christmas, but often they aren't so keen on the associated foods. Banish fruit cake from your tin; instead let them make something they'll enjoy eating too.

TAKES 2 HOURS 20 MINUTES, PLUS COOLING • CUTS INTO 16 SQUARES

200ml/7fl oz sunflower oil, plus extra for greasing
140g/5oz dark chocolate, broken into chunks – standard supermarket chocolate is fine
300g/10oz self-raising flour
300g/10oz light, soft brown sugar
50g/2oz cocoa powder
150ml/¼ pint soured cream
3 eggs
1 tsp vanilla essence

TO DECORATE

250g pack butter, softened
500g box icing sugar, sifted
1–2 tsp peppermint extract
little green food colouring
mint matchstick chocolates and assorted chocolates

1 Heat oven to 160C/140C fan/gas 4 and grease and line a deep 20cm-square cake tin with baking parchment. Whizz the chocolate in a food processor until it makes crumbs (get a grown-up to help).
2 Tip the flour, sugar, cocoa, oil, soured cream, eggs, vanilla and 150ml/¼ pint water into a large mixing bowl. Whisk with an electric whisk until smooth, then stir in the whizzed-up chocolate bits.
3 Scrape into a tin and bake for 1 hour–1 hour 20 minutes, or until a skewer inserted in the centre comes out clean (get a grown-up to help check). Cool.
4 To decorate, put the butter, icing sugar and 1 teaspoon peppermint extract in a big bowl. Beat together with an electric whisk until just smooth. Taste and stir in some more peppermint, if you like, with some green colouring. Spread all over the cooled cake then decorate with the chocolates.

PER SQUARE 632 kcals, protein 5g, carbs 76g, fat 35g, sat fat 15g, fibre 2g, sugar 62g, salt 0.6g

Microwave nutty coffee sponge

The hardest part when cooking with kids can be the waiting time. We've turned this traybake into a microwave-friendly bake to save you tears.

TAKES 25 MINUTES • SERVES 4

85g/3oz very soft butter
85g/3oz golden caster sugar
2 eggs, beaten with a fork
85g/3oz self-raising flour
2 tsp instant coffee powder
small handful walnut pieces (optional)

FOR THE BUTTERCREAM

1 tsp instant coffee powder
1 tsp milk   *Tablespoon, water?*
25g/1oz very soft butter
100g/4oz icing sugar, sifted

1 In a bowl, stir together the butter and sugar with a wooden spoon until light and fluffy (older children and grown-ups can do this with an electric whisk).

2 Gradually add the eggs, followed by the flour and coffee. Stir in most of the nuts (if using), but save a few for decoration. Spread over the base of a small microwaveproof baking dish using a spatula. Cook on High for 2 minutes, then on Medium for 2 minutes.

3 Check to see if the cake is cooked – it should be risen and spring back when touched. If it needs longer, cook on Medium for 1 minute more at a time, until the cake is cooked. Cool.

4 To make the icing, mix the coffee powder in the milk until all the bits dissolve. Tip into a bigger bowl with the butter and icing sugar, and mix with a wooden spoon until smooth (again, use an electric whisk, if you like). Spread over the cake and top with the walnuts you saved, if using.

PER SERVING 538 kcals, protein 7g, carbs 65g, fat 30g, sat fat 16g, fibre 1g, sugar 49g, salt 0.65g

Raspberry–oat traybake

Satisfy your children's cravings for a sweet snack by getting them to help you bake this healthier treat that's packed with good-for-you ingredients.

TAKES 30 MINUTES • CUTS INTO 16 SLICES

50g/2oz butter, plus extra for greasing
150g punnet fresh raspberries
85g/3oz clear honey
200g/7oz rolled oats
50g/2oz ground almonds
½ tsp almond extract

1 Heat oven to 220C/200C fan/gas 7.
2 Use a knob of butter to grease a 20cm- square baking tray. Put the raspberries in a bowl and mash roughly with a fork or potato masher. Set aside.
3 In a medium pan, melt the butter and honey with a pinch of salt. Take it off the heat, then stir in the oats, ground almonds and almond extract. Mix until everything is coated in the butter-and-honey mixture.
4 Use your hands to press half the oat mix in an even layer into the baking tin Spread the mashed raspberries on top, then spoon the remaining oats on top of them and smooth with the back of a spoon. Bake for 10–12 minutes or until golden. Remove from the oven and leave to cool before slicing into 16.

PER SLICE 111 kcals, protein 2g, carbs 13g, fat 6g, sat fat 2g, fibre 1g, sugar 4g, salt 0.06g

Queen of Pudding cakes

Little hands are perfect for adding the finishing touches to these cute cakes. Perfect for really young helpers in the kitchen, for whom icing can still be a bit fiddly.

TAKES 40 MINUTES • CUTS INTO 16 SQUARES

200g/7oz soft butter, plus extra
  for greasing
200g/7oz golden caster sugar
3 eggs
140g/5oz self-raising flour
50g/2oz custard powder
5–6 tbsp raspberry jam
16 mini meringues
icing sugar, to dust

1 Heat oven to 180C/160C fan/gas 4. Put a knob of butter into a 20cm-square baking tin and rub all over to grease with your fingers. Put a square of baking parchment into the bottom of the tin too.

2 Whisk together the butter, sugar, eggs, flour and custard powder until well combined and fluffy (or use an electric whisk, if you can). Spread into the tin with a small spatula and bake for 25–30 minutes until golden and risen. Cool in the tin.

3 Carefully turn the cooled cake out from the tin. Peel off the paper. Spread the top of the cake all over with the jam. Trim the edges using a small serrated knife. Cut into 16 squares with a sharper knife (grown-ups might want to help here). To finish, add a meringue to each mini cake.

PER SQUARE 232 kcals, protein 3g, carbs 31g, fat 12g, sat fat 7g, fibre none, sugar 22g, salt 0.32g

Leftover Halloween-pumpkin-carving cake

Pumpkins can vary dramatically in water content, so keep an eye on the cake towards the end of cooking – yours may take less or more time to cook through.

**TAKES 50 MINUTES • CUTS INTO
15 GENEROUS PORTIONS**

300g/10oz self-raising flour
300g/10oz light muscovado sugar
3 tsp ground mixed spice
2 tsp bicarbonate of soda
175g/6oz sultanas
4 eggs, beaten
200g/7oz butter, melted
zest 1 orange
1 tbsp orange juice
500g/1lb 2oz (peeled weight) pumpkin
  (you can top up with butternut
  squash), grated

FOR DRENCHING AND FROSTING

200g pack cream cheese, at room
  temperature
85g/3oz butter, softened
100g/4oz icing sugar, sifted
zest 1 orange and juice of ½

1 Turn the oven on to 180C/160C fan/gas 4. Butter and line a 30 x 20cm baking tin with baking parchment. Mix the flour, sugar, spice, bicarb and sultanas together in a large bowl.

2 Whisk the eggs with the melted butter, orange zest and juice. Tip into the dry ingredients and mix together. Stir in the grated pumpkin. Spoon into the tin and bake for 30 minutes, or until golden and springy to the touch.

3 Beat together the cream cheese, butter, icing sugar, orange zest and 1 teaspoon of the juice until smooth and creamy – an electric whisk works best, so you can ask a grown-up to do this.

4 When the cake is done, cool for 5 minutes then turn it out of the tin on to a cooling rack. Prick it all over with a skewer and drizzle with the rest of the orange juice. Leave to cool completely.

5 Spread the icing all over the top of the cake with a spatula or cutlery knife.

PER PORTION 408 kcals, protein 5g, carbs 52g, fat 21g, sat fat 13g, fibre 1g, sugar 37g, salt 1.33g

Banana & cinnamon whirls

Based on classic Chelsea buns these smell so heavenly no one will be able to resist.

TAKES 45 MINUTES, PLUS RISING

● **MAKES 9 WHIRLS**

100g/4oz strong white bread flour, plus
    extra for dusting

100g/4oz granary bread flour

½ tsp each salt and caster sugar

½ x 7g sachet yeast

75ml/2½fl oz warm milk

1 egg, beaten with a fork

1 tbsp sunflower oil

50ml/2fl oz water.

25g/1oz unsalted butter, melted, plus
    extra for greasing

2 very ripe medium-size bananas,
    thinly sliced

100g/4oz dried apricots, chopped

1 tsp ground cinnamon

50g/2oz light muscovado sugar

2 tbsp clear honey

1 Combine both the flours, the salt, caster sugar and yeast in a bowl. Make a hole in the middle. Mix the milk with half the egg and the oil, then stir in the water.

2 Pour the milky mixture into the hole and mix. Knead the dough for 10 minutes on a floured surface. Lift into an oiled bowl, cover, and leave to rise somewhere warm until doubled in size, then roll on a floured surface until about 30 x 25cm – use a ruler. Brush with melted butter.

4 Mix together the bananas, apricots, cinnamon and muscovado sugar, and scatter all over the dough. Roll up the dough from one of the long sides. Pinch the ends together. Ask a grown-up to cut it into 9 pieces. Lift the slices whirly-side into a buttered 20cm-square baking tin. Cover and leave for 30 minutes to rise.

5 Heat oven to 200C/180C fan/gas 6. Brush the leftover egg over the buns then bake for 20–25 minutes. Brush the tops with the honey.

PER WHIRL 191 kcals, protein 5g, carbs 36g, fat 4g, sat fat 2g, fibre 2g, sugar 18g, salt 0.32g

Date & apple squares

The apple adds a lovely sweetness to these oaty bars – and don't worry if your children don't like dates, they won't even notice them once they're all mashed up.

TAKES 55 MINUTES • CUTS INTO 8 SQUARES

225g/8oz butter, plus extra for greasing
140g/5oz cooking apples, peeled, cored and chopped
140g/5oz stoned dates, chopped
300g/10oz light soft brown sugar
175g/6oz plain flour
1 tsp bicarbonate of soda
100g/4oz porridge oats

1 Heat oven to 190C/170C fan/gas 5. Rub a knob of butter around an 18cm-square cake tin and put a square of baking parchment in the bottom.

2 Tip the apples into a pan with 2 tablespoons water. Bring to the boil and simmer on a low heat for 5 minutes until tender and slightly pulpy. Add the dates and 50g of the sugar, and cook for a further 5 minutes. Take off the heat and use a potato masher to mash the fruit together. Set aside.

3 Gently melt the butter in a pan. Mix the flour, bicarb, oats and remaining sugar in a bowl. Pour in the melted butter and stir until the oats are coated.

4 Press half the mixture firmly into the tin, then use a spoon to spread the apple mix on top. Cover with the remaining oat mixture and press down. Bake for 30–35 minutes until golden and firm. Cool in the tin before cutting into 8 squares.

PER SQUARE 513 kcals, protein 5g, carbs 68g, fat 24g, sat fat 15g, fibre 4g, sugar 47g, salt 0.8g

Pretzel–popcorn squares

The different crunchy textures in these chewy snacks, all held together with melted marshmallows, is so very moreish you won't stop at one. Yum!

TAKES 15 MINUTES • CUTS INTO 12 SQUARES

300g/10oz marshmallows
200g/7oz pretzels
140g/5oz plain popcorn

1 Line a roughly 23 x 33cm cake tin with baking parchment. Put the marshmallows into a pan and melt, stirring continuously with a wooden spoon (you could get a grown-up to do this bit).

2 Put the pretzels into a big plastic food bag and sit the bag on a chopping board. Use the end of a rolling pin to bash the pretzels into chunky pieces – but not crumbs!

3 Take the marshmallows off the heat and stir in the popcorn and pretzels. Pour into the tin and put in the fridge to set. Cut into 12 squares with a sharp knife to serve (get a grown-up to do this bit for you).

PER SQUARE 214 kcals, protein 3g, carbs 38g, fat 6g, sat fat 1g, fibre none, sugar 16g, salt 0.7g

Breakfast bars

This fruity, chewy bar is packed with delicious ingredients – perfect to pack into school lunchboxes.

TAKES 45 MINUTES • CUTS INTO 12 BARS

50g/2oz mixed dried fruit (a mixture of raisins, sultanas and apricots is nice)
50g/2oz mixed seeds
140g/5oz oats
25g/1oz multi-grain hoop cereal
100g/4oz butter
100g/4oz light muscovado sugar
100g/4oz golden syrup

1 First get the tin ready. Line the base of a 20cm-square cake tin with a square of baking parchment. Heat oven to 160C/140C fan/gas 3.

2 Put the dried fruit in a mixing bowl. Add the seeds, oats and cereal, and mix well.

3 Put the butter, sugar and golden syrup in a pan. Cook gently on the hob, stirring with the spatula, until the butter and sugar are melted. Take the pan off the heat and pour the dry ingredients into the pan. Mix well until all the ingredients are coated with the syrup mix.

4 Fill the baking tin with the mixture, using a spatula to press it down evenly. Put the tin in the oven and bake for 20 minutes, then leave to cool completely before cutting into 12 bars. Store in an airtight tin for up to 3 days – if they last that long!

PER BAR 205 kcals, protein 3g, carbs 25g, fat 10g, sat fat 5g, fibre 2g, sugar 17g, salt 0.2g

Pink jam slice

This fun, crumbly slice will be a hit at birthday parties. You can use your favourite jam and dye the icing so that it is the same colour.

TAKES 1 HOUR, PLUS COOLING AND SETTING • CUTS INTO 20 PIECES

400g/14oz butter, at room temperature
120g/4½oz golden caster sugar
2 tsp vanilla extract
1 large egg yolk
500g/1lb 2oz plain flour
400g/14oz raspberry jam
500g/1lb 2oz icing sugar
pink food colouring

1 Heat oven to 180C/160C fan/gas 4. Line a 20 x 30cm tin with baking parchment.
2 Beat the butter, caster sugar, vanilla and egg yolk together in a large bowl until pale. Stir in the flour with a good pinch of salt. Use your hands to bring together to a crumbly dough.
3 Press half the mixture into the base of the tin, as evenly as you can, smoothing the top. Spread over the jam, leaving a 1cm/½in empty border all around the edge. Crumble over the remaining shortbread mixture, then pat down – trying not to dislodge the jam too much. Bake for 35 minutes until pale golden. Cool in the tin.
4 Sift the icing sugar into a bowl, and stir in about 100ml/3½fl oz water with some food colouring, to a thick but runny icing. Pour over the slice, then spread evenly. Quickly dot over some more food colouring, then use a skewer to swirl and marble the top. Leave to set for 1 hour.

PER SLICE 412 kcals, protein 3g, carbs 63g, fat 17g, sat fat 11g, fibre 1g, sugar 44g, salt 0.3g

Easy Simnel cake

This easy twist on the classic cake will see you through several rounds of tea. Add 11 marzipan 'Apostles' to be traditional, or you could make 15, so each square gets one.

TAKES 1 HOUR 40 MINUTES, PLUS SOAKING • CUTS INTO 15 SQUARES

250g/9oz mixed dried fruit

100g/4oz dried apricots, chopped

85g/3oz glacé cherries, chopped

zest 2 oranges, juice 1 orange (use the second in the topping)

200g/7oz butter, softened, plus extra for greasing

200g/7oz light muscovado sugar

4 large eggs

200g/7oz self-raising flour

50g/2oz ground almonds

2 tsp each ground mixed spice and ground cinnamon

500g/1lb 2oz marzipan, 200g/7oz cut into 2cm/¾in chunks, 100g/4oz rolled into 11 balls for the topping

FOR THE TOPPING

50g/2oz each butter and light muscovado sugar

100g/4oz each plain flour and flaked almonds

3 tbsp golden syrup

85g/3oz icing sugar, sifted

2–3 tsp orange juice

1 Soak all of the dried fruit in orange juice overnight.

2 Butter and line a 20 x 30cm tin with baking parchment. Heat oven to 160C/140C fan/gas 3. In a large bowl beat the butter and sugar with an electric whisk. Add the eggs one at a time, then the flour, ground almonds and spices. Stir in the marzipan chunks, zest, dried fruit and any remaining juice.

3 Scrape the mixture into the tin, level the surface and bake for 45 minutes. Remove from the oven and increase heat to 200C/180C fan/gas 6.

4 Rub the butter, sugar and flour for the topping together. Grate in the remaining 200g/7oz marzipan. Mix in the flaked almonds and syrup with a fork. Sprinkle over the cake and bake for 12–15 minutes.

5 Arrange the marzipan balls on top and cool in the tin. Mix the icing sugar with orange juice to give a runny icing, drizzle over the cake, leave to set, then slice.

PER SQUARE 576 kcals, protein 9g, carbs 79g, fat 25g, sat fat 10g, fibre 3g, sugar 65g, salt 0.5g

Lemon & lavender fondant fancies

Classic fondant fancies take some skill and patience to decorate, but it's worth it.

TAKES 1¾ HOURS, PLUS CHILLING

● **MAKES 16**

175g/6oz butter, softened
250g/9oz caster sugar
3 large eggs
100g/4oz full-fat natural yogurt
300g/10oz plain flour
1½ tsp baking powder

FOR THE BUTTERCREAM

1 tsp dried lavender, ground to a
    powder, plus extra to decorate
100g/4oz butter
100g/4oz icing sugar
zest 1 lemon, plus a little to decorate

FOR THE FONDANT ICING

8 tbsp apricot jam, heated then sifted
1kg pack fondant icing sugar, sifted
yellow and purple food colouring

1 Heat oven to 160C/140C fan/gas 3. Line a 20cm-square tin with parchment. Beat the butter, sugar, eggs, yogurt, flour and baking powder together. Scrape into the tin and bake for 45–50 minutes until cooked. Cool.

2 Beat together the butter and icing sugar. Halve, add lavender to one and zest to the other. Transfer to piping bags.

3 Slice the rounded top off the cake. Flip over, trim the edges, and cut into 16 squares. Brush with jam. Pipe half with a dome of lemon buttercream, half with lavender. Chill for 1 hour.

4 Mix water into fondant icing sugar until thick but pourable. Spoon a little into a piping bag for later. Halve the remaining icing, dye one yellow and the other lilac.

5 Transfer the sponges to a wire rack set over a tin. Spoon icing over each sponge – lilac for the lavender fancies and yellow for the lemon, covering fully. Pipe with the reserved white icing and decorate with lemon zest and lavender.

PER FANCY 526 kcals, protein 4g, carbs 92g, fat 16g, sat fat 9g, fibre 1g, sugar 81g, salt 0.5g

Coconut-ice marshmallows

This recipe makes two variations, but you can stick to just one colour, if you prefer.

TAKES 50 MINUTES, PLUS SETTING
- **MAKES 40–50 DEPENDING ON THE SIZE**

300g/10oz desiccated coconut, half toasted in a pan
10 sheets leaf gelatine, soaked in cold water for 10 minutes
500g/1lb 2oz granulated sugar
4 tsp liquid glucose
2 large egg whites
1 tsp vanilla extract
1 tbsp Malibu or coconut liqueur
pink food colouring
a little icing sugar, for dusting

1 Line two square tins (18cm) with baking parchment. Spread half the toasted coconut over the base of one, and half the untoasted coconut over the other.

2 Melt the sugar, glucose and 200ml/7fl oz cold water over a low heat in a small, deep, heavy-based pan. Increase the heat and boil until it reaches firm-ball stage on a sugar thermometer (125C).

3 Meanwhile, beat the egg whites in a bowl with an electric whisk until stiff.

4 Pour the sugar syrup in a steady stream into the egg whites while whisking. Squeeze the excess water from the gelatine and add, one at a time. Add the vanilla and Malibu, and whisk for 10 minutes. Spread half into the toasted coconut tin, then sprinkle over the toasted coconut.

5 Whisk pink food colouring into the remaining mix. Scrape into the other tin, and sprinkle with the untoasted coconut. Set until firm, then cut into squares.

PER MARSHMALLOW (50) 80 kcals, protein 1g, carbs 11g, fat 4g, sat fat 3g, fibre 1g, sugar 11g, salt none

Festive fruitcake fancies

This clever square fruitcake neatly divides into four smaller versions for decorating and giving to your loved ones over Christmas.

TAKES 2 HOURS, PLUS COOLING ●
MAKES 4 SMALL CAKES, FOR GIFTING
200g/7oz dark muscovado sugar
175g/6oz butter, diced, plus extra
    for greasing
800g/1lb 10 oz mixed, luxury dried fruit
zest and juice 1 orange
100ml/4fl oz sherry
3 large eggs, beaten
85g/3oz ground almonds
200g/7oz plain flour
½ tsp baking powder
1 tbsp ground mixed spice
400g/14oz marzipan, quartered
1kg pack fondant icing sugar
½ x 340g jar apricot jam, warmed
    and sifted
food colouring (optional)
sugared almonds, mini white
    marshmallows, sprinkles, mini
    gingerbread men or candy canes,
    to decorate

1 Tip the sugar, butter, fruit, orange zest and juice and sherry into a large pan. Bring to the boil, then bubble gently for 10 minutes, stirring occasionally. Cool.
2 Heat oven to 150C/130C fan/gas 2. Line the base and sides of an 18cm-square tin with baking parchment.
3 Stir the eggs, almonds, flour, baking powder and spice into the fruit. Spoon into the tin, level and bake for 45 minutes. Lower oven to 140C/120C fan/gas 1 and cook for 1 hour. Cool.
4 Trim the cake edges, then quarter. Roll out each piece of marzipan on a surface dusted with icing sugar. Brush the cakes with jam, then cover each with marzipan, trimming the excess at the base.
5 Sift the remaining icing sugar, and mix in enough water to give a runny but thick icing. Dye, if you like. Sit the cakes on a wire rack over a tin and spoon over icing to cover. Leave to set, then decorate.

PER CAKE 2809 kcals, protein 27g, carbs 528g, fat 66g, sat fat 26g, fibre 8g, sugar 488g, salt 1.5g

Malty chocolate birthday cake

From 8 years old to 80 years old – anyone would love this yummy, but deceptively easy cake for their special celebration.

TAKES 45 MINUTES • CUTS INTO 12 SQUARES

140g/5oz soft butter, plus extra for greasing
175g/6oz golden caster sugar
2 large eggs
225g/8oz self-raising wholemeal flour
50g/2oz cocoa powder
50g/2oz malt drinking powder (like Horlicks)
¼ tsp bicarbonate of soda
250g/9oz natural yogurt

TO DECORATE

300g/10oz golden icing sugar, sifted
2 tbsp cocoa powder, sifted
1 tbsp butter, melted
3–4 tbsp boiling water
50g/2oz each milk, dark and white chocolate, broken into squares

1 Heat oven to 180C/160C fan/gas 4. Butter and line the base of an 18 x 28cm traybake tin. Beat the butter and sugar with an electric hand whisk until fluffy. Add the eggs a little at a time.

2 Tip the flour, cocoa, malt powder and bicarbonate of soda into the bowl and pour in the yogurt. Stir to a smooth mixture and spoon into the tin. Bake for 20–25 minutes. Cool in the tin for 5 minutes, then cool on a wire rack.

3 For the icing, sift the icing sugar and cocoa into a bowl, then pour in the butter and 2 tablespoons just-boiled water. Stir together to a smooth consistency. Spread over the top of the cake.

4 Melt the chocolates in three bowls in the microwave on High for 1 minute or over a pan of simmering water. Spoon the melted chocolates into three piping bags. Snip the ends off and pipe 12 simple shapes on top of the cake. Leave to set. Cut into 12 squares.

PER SQUARE 432 kcals, protein 6g, carbs 65g, fat 18g, sat fat 10g, fibre 3g, sugar 51g, salt 0.4g

Autumn toffee-apple cake

This Bonfire Night-inspired cake is a great twist on traditional toffee apples. Enjoy with a cuppa or warm with cream and extra toffee sauce – yummy!

TAKES 1¾ HOURS, PLUS COOLING

- **CUTS INTO 15 SQUARES**

250g/9oz butter, softened, plus extra for greasing

200g/7oz dates, roughly chopped

200ml/7fl oz milk, plus a splash

300g/10oz self-raising flour

200g/7oz light soft brown sugar

½ tsp baking powder

4 large eggs

1 tbsp each ground mixed spice and ground ginger

1 tsp vanilla extract

3 small red apples

squeeze lemon juice

handful toffees

a little icing sugar, for dusting

1 Heat oven to 180C/160C fan/gas 4. Grease and line a 20 x 30cm traybake tin with baking parchment. Bring the dates and milk to a simmer. Remove from the heat and set aside for 15 minutes.

2 Whizz the date mixture to a purée in a food processor, then scrape into a large mixing bowl. Add the butter, flour, brown sugar, baking powder, eggs, spices and vanilla, but don't mix yet.

3 Quarter and core the apples, then slice thinly, tossing them in lemon juice as you go. Beat together the cake ingredients with an electric whisk, then scrape into the tin. Arrange the apple slices, overlapping, on top of the cake. Bake for 45–50 minutes until a skewer inserted comes out clean. Cool in the tin.

4 Put the toffees in a small pan with a splash of milk and gently melt, stirring, until runny. To finish, dust with a little icing sugar, then drizzle sauce all over the cake. Cut into squares or slices to serve.

PER SQUARE 327 kcals, protein 5g, carbs 42g, fat 17g, sat fat 10g, fibre 2g, sugar 27g, salt 0.53g

Pick & mix love lamingtons

Perfect for a wedding; all you need is love … hearts to make these cute cakes. This recipe makes 15, so bake as many batches as you need for your guests.

TAKES 2 HOURS 25 MINUTES
● **MAKES 15**

250g pack softened butter, plus extra
   for greasing
300g/10oz self-raising flour
250g/9oz caster sugar
¼ tsp baking powder
4 large eggs
150g pot natural yogurt
1 tsp vanilla extract
jar lemon curd, seedless raspberry jam
   or lime marmalade, or a mixture
140g/5oz desiccated coconut
bag of love hearts and 15 roughly
   10cm/4in squares of pretty paper

1 Heat oven to 180C/160C fan/gas 4. Grease and line a 20 x 30cm traybake tin with baking parchment. Beat the butter, flour, sugar, baking powder, eggs, yogurt and vanilla together with an electric whisk until lump-free. Spoon into the tin and bake for 25 minutes until a skewer poked in to the cake comes out clean. Cool on a wire rack.

2 Trim the edges off the sponge, then cut into 15 roughly 5cm/2in squares. Warm the jam or marmalade until runny, if using these instead of curd, sieving the marmalade of its bits. Tip the coconut on to a tray. Brush each square on the top and sides with either curd, jam or marmalade – then dip into the coconut.

3 Can be made the day before and stored in airtight containers. Top with love hearts and sit on squares of coloured paper to serve.

PER LAMINGTON 401 kcals, protein 5g, carbs 47g, fat 23g, sat fat 15g, fibre 2g, sugar 33g, salt 0.51g

Sugar-dusted passion cake

This is a cross between a carrot cake and a hummingbird cake – a tropical fruity bake very popular in New Zealand and Australia.

TAKES 1 HOUR 20 MINUTES
● **CUTS INTO 12 SQUARES**

250ml/9fl oz sunflower oil
140g/5oz dark muscovado sugar, sifted
250g/9oz wholemeal flour
100g/4oz desiccated coconut
2 tsp each ground mixed spice and
   baking powder
50g/2oz walnuts, roughly chopped
4 large eggs, lightly beaten with a fork
3 tsp vanilla extract
250g/9oz carrots, peeled and grated
432g can crushed pineapple, drained,
   reserving 50ml/2fl oz juice
zest and juice 2 limes
200g/7oz caster sugar
icing sugar, to dust
mascarpone and natural yogurt,
   to serve

1 Heat oven to 160C/140C fan/gas 3. Line a deep 20cm-square tin with baking parchment. Mix together the sugar, flour, coconut, mixed spice, baking powder and walnuts. Whisk together the oil, eggs and 2 teaspoons of the vanilla extract, then pour over the dry ingredients. Add the carrots, pineapple, reserved pineapple juice and zest, and mix. Scrape into the tin and bake for 1 hour.

2 Meanwhile, make a syrup by gently heating the caster sugar, lime juice and a teaspoon of vanilla in a pan. Once dissolved, boil for 3 minutes until syrupy.

3 Once cool enough to handle, turn the cake on to a wire rack. Using a skewer, poke holes all over the cake and drizzle over the syrup a little at a time. Cool.

4 Trim the edges and dust with icing sugar (use a paper doily as a stencil if you like). Try mixing equal amounts of mascarpone and natural yogurt with a little more icing sugar to serve alongside.

PER SQUARE 487 kcals, protein 7g, carbs 50g, fat 30g, sat fat 8g, fibre 4g, sugar 36g, salt 0.36g

Christmas brownies

Cranberries and spiced mincemeat gives these gooey brownies a festive twist. Enjoy warm with ice cream for pud, or allow to cool and firm up before slicing.

TAKES 1½ HOURS • CUTS INTO 16 SLICES

100g/4oz unsalted butter, diced, plus extra for greasing

200g bar dark chocolate, broken into squares

3 large eggs

250g/9oz golden caster sugar

100g/4oz plain flour

3 tbsp cocoa powder

50g/2oz dried cranberries

100g/4oz pecan nuts, roughly chopped

175g/6oz mincemeat

icing sugar (optional), to dust

1 Heat oven to 180C/160C fan/gas 4. Grease and line a deep 20cm square tin with baking parchment. Put the butter and chocolate in a heatproof bowl and melt over a pan of simmering water. Cool slightly.

2 Using an electric whisk, whisk the eggs and sugar together until pale and thick enough to hold a trail when the beaters are lifted. Carefully fold the chocolate mixture into the egg mixture. Sift the flour and cocoa together over the mixture and gently fold these in, too. Fold in the dried cranberries, pecans and mincemeat.

3 Tip the mixture into the prepared baking tin. Bake for 40–45 minutes until nicely crusted but still soft in the middle. Cool and sprinkle with icing sugar to serve, if you like.

PER BROWNIE 300 kcals, protein 4g, carbs 37g, fat 15g, sat fat 6g, fibre 2g, sugar 33g, salt 0.2g

Easter cherry slice

This teatime treat is a cross between a fruity Simnel cake and a Bakewell tart – a lovely bake to welcome guests over the Bank Holiday.

TAKES 1 HOUR 50 MINUTES, PLUS CHILLING • CUTS INTO 15 SQUARES

75g/2½oz self-raising flour, plus extra for dusting
375g pack sweet shortcrust pastry
140g/5oz butter, softened
140g/5oz golden caster sugar
2 large eggs
75g/2½oz ground almonds
175g/6oz mixed dried fruit
50g/2oz glacé cherries, halved
zest and juice 1 orange
1 tsp each ground mixed spice and ground cinnamon
6 tbsp cherry jam
350g/12oz marzipan, ½ cut into small cubes, ½ rolled into 11 balls to represent the Apostles
50g/2oz icing sugar
25g/1oz flaked toasted almonds

1 Roll out the pastry and use to line a 20 x 30cm tin. Chill for at least 30 minutes.
2 Heat oven to 200C/180C fan/gas 6. Line the pastry with baking paper and fill with baking beans. Blind-bake for 15 minutes, remove the beans and parchment, and bake for 10 minutes more until biscuity.
3 Reduce oven to 170C/150C fan/gas 3½. Beat the butter and sugar until creamy. Add the eggs, one at a time, then stir in the flour, almonds, dried fruit, cherries, half the zest and the spices. Spread the jam over the base of the tart, then dot over the cubes of marzipan. Spread over the cake mixture, then bake for 35 minutes until golden. Cool in the tin.
4 Brown the tops of the marzipan balls under the grill. Mix the icing sugar with orange juice to make a thick, smooth icing. Drizzle over the tart, top with the marzipan balls, flaked almonds and the remaining orange zest. Cut into squares.

PER SQUARE 448 kcals, protein 6g, carbs 56g, fat 22g, sat fat 8g, fibre 1g, sugar 42g, salt 0.5g

Christmas buns

There might be nothing nicer than freshly baked Chelsea buns, and these festive versions make for a perfect Christmas Day breakfast with a mug of tea.

TAKES 1 HOUR, PLUS RISING

● **MAKES 9**

500g bag strong white flour, plus extra
    for dusting

7g sachet fact-action dried yeast

300ml/10fl oz milk

50g/2oz unsalted butter, softened

1 egg

vegetable oil, for greasing

FOR THE FILLING

25g/1oz unsalted butter, melted

85g/3oz soft brown sugar

2 tsp ground cinnamon

100g/4oz dried cranberries

100g/4oz chopped dried apricots

FOR THE ICING

200g/7oz icing sugar

zest 1 lemon or orange

1 Mix the flour, yeast and 1 teaspoon salt in a large bowl. Warm the milk and butter in a pan until the butter melts and the mixture is lukewarm. Add with the egg to the flour mixture and stir to a soft dough.

2 Knead the dough for 5 minutes, until no longer sticky. Leave to double in size somewhere warm in an oiled bowl, covered with oiled clingfilm.

3 Knead the dough for 30 seconds. Roll into a 2cm/¾in-thick rectangle. Brush all over with the melted butter, then sprinkle over the sugar, cinnamon and fruit.

4 Roll up the dough like a Swiss roll, cut into nine slices and arrange in an oiled tin, leaving a little space between each. Cover with a tea towel and leave to rise for 30 minutes.

5 Heat oven to 190C/170C fan/gas 5. Bake for 20–25 minutes.

6 Once cool, mix the icing sugar, zest with 2 tablespoons water, and drizzle over the buns.

PER BUN 454 kcals, protein 8g, carbs 87g, fat 9g, sat fat 5g, fibre 4g, sugar 45g, salt 0.65g

Fruity flag traybake

This makes a patriotic and impressive centrepiece for any sporting occasion, but being a traybake it is much simpler than it looks.

TAKES 1¼ HOURS ● CUTS INTO 15 SQUARES

FOR THE SPONGE

100g/4oz butter softened, plus extra for greasing
175g/6oz self-raising flour
50g/2oz ground almonds
1 tsp baking powder
4 large eggs
200g/7oz caster sugar
100g/4oz full-fat Greek yogurt
1 tsp vanilla extract

FOR THE BUTTER ICING

175g/6oz butter, softened
350g/12oz icing sugar, sifted
1 tsp vanilla extract

TO DECORATE

about 300g/10oz raspberries
about 175g/6oz blueberries

1 Heat oven to 180C/160C fan/gas 4. Butter and line a 30 x 20cm traybake tin with baking parchment. Measure all the sponge ingredients into a mixing bowl and mix together using an electric hand whisk until smooth. Spoon into the tin and level the surface. Bake for 25–30 minutes until a skewer poked in to the centre comes out clean. Transfer to a wire rack to cool then remove the baking parchment.

2 To make the icing, beat the butter, icing sugar and vanilla together with an electric whisk until light and fluffy. Spread the icing over the top of the cold cake.

3 To decorate, put a double row of raspberries across the centre and down the length of the cake to make a cross. Next, place a single row diagonally from each corner to the middle. Now fill in the empty spaces with blueberries. Cut into 15 squares to serve.

PER SQUARE 390 kcals, protein 4g, carbs 49g, fat 20g, sat fat 11g, fibre 1g, sugar 41g, salt 0.6g

Starry mincemeat slices

Fancy a change from mince pies? This fun, festive alternative is super-simple to assemble but looks really cute with its cut-out star pattern.

TAKES 55 MINUTES, PLUS CHILLING

● **CUTS INTO 12**

butter, for greasing

2 x 410g jars mincemeat

175g/6oz grated Bramley apple, squeezed to remove excess juice

2 x 375g packs ready-rolled shortcrust pastry sheets

white caster sugar, for dredging

1 Butter a 30 x 20cm traybake tin. Mix the mincemeat and grated apple. Unroll the pastry sheets. Lift one sheet into the tin so that the pastry lines it and the excess hangs over the sides. Spread the mincemeat mix over evenly.

2 Leave the other sheet on its wrapping, but lightly mark the size of the tin on to it. Stamp out stars, spaced apart, and set aside – don't go outside the markings. Carefully invert the pastry on top of the mincemeat, pastry-side down, and peel off the wrapping. Press the edges together around the edge of the tin, trim the excess, then randomly put the cut-out stars over the pastry.

3 Chill for 20 minutes. Meanwhile, heat oven to 200C/180C fan/gas 6 with a large baking sheet inside it. Dredge the pastry with sugar and bake the tart on the hot baking sheet for 30 minutes until golden. Remove and dredge with more sugar.

PER SLICE 481 kcals, protein 4g, carbs 74g, fat 21g, sat fat 9g, fibre 2g, sugar 45g, salt 0.67g

Blueberry & cream layer cake

This Norwegian cake is perfect for a big gathering or a birthday party. Use a little sherry or cassis instead of the milk for a more grown-up taste.

TAKES 1 HOUR 5 MINUTES, PLUS COOLING • SERVES 18

butter, for greasing
10 eggs, beaten
300g/10oz golden caster sugar
300g/10oz plain flour mixed with 2 tsp baking powder
2 tbsp blueberry or strawberry jam
1 litre/1¾ pints double cream
1 tsp vanilla extract
1 tbsp icing sugar
100ml/3½fl oz milk
3 x 180g packs blueberries

1 Heat oven to 190C/170C fan/gas 5. Line a 20 x 30cm traybake tin – the lining paper should come up 2.5cm/1in above the edge of the tin. In a large bowl, whisk the eggs and sugar for 8–10 minutes until the mixture is pale and thickened.

2 Use a metal spoon to gently fold in the flour. Pour this into the baking tin and bake for 35 minutes until cooked. Cool on a wire rack.

3 Once cool, divide into three layers. Mix the jam with 1 tablespoon warm water and whip the cream with the vanilla and icing sugar until it holds its shape.

4 Drizzle one cake layer with one-third of the milk. Spread with some jam, then cream, then scatter over 1 pack of blueberries. Cover with the second layer of sponge and repeat the toppings. Put the third layer of sponge on top and drizzle over the remaining milk, spread the whipped cream and dot the remaining pack of blueberries on top.

PER SERVING 478 kcals, protein 8g, carbs 36g, fat 35g, sat fat 18g, fibre 1g, sugar 23g, salt 0.3g

Parkin

This traditional Yorkshire bake needs to mature before eating, so it's the perfect make-ahead treat for Bonfire Night.

TAKES 1½ HOURS • CUTS INTO 16 SQUARES

140g/5oz butter, plus extra for greasing
100g/4oz light soft brown sugar
100g/4oz golden syrup
100g/4oz treacle
250g/9oz plain flour
175g/6oz oatmeal (fine or medium, depending on how you like it)
1 tbsp ground ginger
1 tbsp ground mixed spice
1 tsp bicarbonate of soda
1 large egg, beaten
150ml/¼ pint milk

1 Heat oven to 160C/140C fan/gas 3. Grease and line a deep 20cm-square tin with baking parchment. Put the butter, sugar, golden syrup and treacle in a pan and heat gently until all melted together.
2 Mix the flour, oatmeal, spices and bicarb in a big bowl. Stir in the warm syrupy mixture, then whisk together the egg and milk, and stir this in too. Scrape into the tin and bake for 50–60 minutes until a skewer poked in to the centre comes out with just a few damp crumbs, not wet batter.
3 Cool, then wrap loosely in parchment and put in a cake tin for at least a day, but better two, before cutting into 16 squares and eating.

PER SQUARE 229 kcals, protein 4g, carbs 35g, fat 9g, sat fat 5g, fibre 1g, sugar 16g, salt 0.4g

Simnel tart

If you want to knock up a pudding in a hurry for after the Easter lunch, this simple traybake tart fits the bill. Just five ingredients, then serve with ice cream or custard.

TAKES 35 MINUTES ● SERVES 4
200g/7oz mixed dried fruit
zest and juice 1 small orange
375g sheet ready-rolled puff pastry
3 tbsp apricot jam
200g/7oz marzipan, grated
ice cream or custard, to serve

1 Mix the dried fruit and orange zest and juice in a bowl. Find a traybake tin that will fit the unrolled pastry snugly, then line with baking parchment. Lay in the pastry. Mark a border 2cm/¾in from the edge with a knife, brush the jam over the inside section, then chill for at least 10 minutes, or as long as you want.
2 Heat oven to 220C/200C fan/gas 7. Drain the fruit, then stir in the marzipan. Scatter the fruit mix inside the border. Bake for 20 minutes, until the pastry is golden, then immediately cut into squares and serve.

PER SERVING 713 kcals, protein 9g, carbs 112g, fat 29g, sat fat 9g, fibre 2g, sugar 78g, salt 0.84g

Blackberry & apple mallow traybake

This gorgeous fruity sponge needs no icing, instead a little berry-rippled meringue is baked onto each portion.

TAKES 1½ HOURS • MAKES 16 SQUARES

140g/5oz unsalted butter, softened, plus a little for greasing
140g/5oz golden caster sugar
1 egg and 2 yolks, beaten together
1 tsp each vanilla extract, baking powder and freshly grated nutmeg
100g/4oz self-raising flour
100g/4oz ground almonds
1 large Bramley apple (about 200g/7oz), peeled and sliced
125g/4½oz blackberries

FOR THE MALLOW AND BERRY PURÉE

25g/1oz blackberries
100g/4oz white caster sugar, plus 1 tsp
2 egg whites
1 tsp lemon juice
1–2 tbsp toasted flaked almonds
a little icing sugar, to dust

1 Microwave 25g berries and 1 teaspoon sugar for 30 seconds on High in a cling-filmed bowl. Mash the fruit, then cool.

2 Heat oven to 160C/140C fan/gas 3. Grease and line the base and sides of a deep 23cm square tin. Beat the butter, sugar, eggs and vanilla until pale and creamy. Fold in the flour, almonds, baking powder, nutmeg and a pinch of salt.

3 Fold in the apple, then spread the mixture into the tin. Scatter with the 125g/4½oz berries, push in a little, then bake for 45 minutes until a skewer poked in comes out clean. Leave the oven on.

4 For the mallow, beat the egg whites and lemon juice to stiff peaks. Beat in the sugar, 1 tablespoon at a time, until stiff. Ripple with the berry purée, then spoon into a piping bag fitted with a 1cm nozzle. Pipe 16 walnut-sized meringues on top of the cake, scatter with almonds, and bake for 10 minutes until the meringues are just set. Cool, then dust with icing sugar.

PER SQUARE 207 kcals, protein 3g, carbs 21g, fat 12g, sat fat 5g, fibre 1g, sugar 17g, salt 0.2g

Cranberry, pumpkin seed & caramel flapjacks

Don't be tempted to use unsalted butter here, as you need the added salt to balance the sweetness from the caramel and dried fruit.

TAKES 55 MINUTES • MAKES 16

250g pack salted butter
6 tbsp caramel, from a 397g can caramel (use remainder for topping, see below)
50g/2oz golden caster sugar
350g/12oz rolled oats
85g/3oz self-raising flour

FOR THE TOPPING

remaining 300g/10oz caramel
50g/2oz salted butter
25g/1oz pumpkin seeds
50g/2oz dried cranberries
25g/1oz dark chocolate chips

1 Heat oven to 160C/140C fan/gas 3 and line a 22cm square cake tin with baking parchment. Melt the butter, caramel and sugar in a large saucepan, then tip in the oats and flour. Stir well, making sure every oat is covered in the buttery mixture, then tip into your cake tin and press down firmly with the back of a spoon to level the surface. Bake for 40 minutes.

2 Tip the remaining caramel and the butter into a small saucepan, and bubble for 5 minutes, stirring continuously, until the mixture turns dark golden brown and thickens a little. When the flapjacks have finished cooking, remove them from the oven and pour over the hot caramel. Leave to cool for 5 minutes, then scatter with the seeds, cranberries and chocolate chips. Leave to cool completely in the tin before cutting into squares.

PER FLAPJACK 318 kcals, protein 5g, carbs 30g, fat 19g, sat fat 11g, fibre 3g, sugar 13g, salt 0.4g

Fudgy fig roll

The flavours of the traditional biscuit are turned into a squidgy Swiss roll – perfect with a pot of tea.

TAKES 1¼ HOURS, PLUS SOFTENING AND COOLING • CUTS INTO 10 SLICES

140g/5oz soft dried figs, chopped and soaked in boiling water for 30 minutes
1 medium, very ripe banana
knob butter, for greasing
3 large eggs, separated
225g/8oz light muscovado sugar
120g/4½oz wholemeal flour
1 tsp bicarbonate of soda
1 tsp ground cinnamon
good grating fresh nutmeg
4 tbsp golden caster sugar

FOR THE FILLING

300ml/½ pint double cream
4 tbsp icing sugar, sifted
about 250–300g fig jam or conserve

1 Drain the figs and mash with the banana.

2 Heat oven to 190C/170C fan/gas 5. Grease a shallow 34 x 24cm tin and line with baking parchment. Beat the egg whites to stiff peaks then add half the muscovado sugar and beat until glossy.

3 In another bowl, beat the yolks with the remaining sugar until pale. Whisk in the mashed fig mix. Gently fold this mixture into the meringue mixture. Mix the flour, bicarbonate of soda, spices and a pinch of salt, sprinkle and gently fold in until well combined. Spread into the tin and bake for 12–15 minutes until springy.

4 Scatter caster sugar over a clean tea towel, flip on the cake, peel off the parchment, then roll up from the shortest side with the tea towel inside. Cool.

5 Unroll gently. Whisk the cream and icing sugar to soft peaks. Spread the jam over the cake, then the cream. Roll up again and slice.

PER SLICE 456 kcals, protein 5g, carbs 67g, fat 19g, sat fat 11g, fibre 3g, sugar 60g, salt 0.4g

Salted caramel & peanut butter billionaire's slice

Crunchy peanut biscuit base, oozing salted caramel and sticky peanut butter, all topped off with rich, dark chocolate. Do we need to say any more?

TAKES 1 HOUR 40 MINUTES, PLUS CHILLING • CUTS INTO 15 BIG SLICES OR 20 SMALLER ONES

FOR THE BASE

225g/8oz butter, chopped into cubes
140g/5oz unsalted peanuts, toasted and cooled
225g/8oz plain flour
50g/2oz cornflour
85g/3oz golden caster sugar

FOR THE PEANUT LAYER

140g/5oz butter
140g/5oz icing sugar, sifted
225g/8oz smooth peanut butter

FOR THE CARAMEL LAYER

2 x 397g cans Carnation caramel
1½ tsp flaky sea salt

FOR THE CHOC-TOFFEE TOP

140g/5oz soft dairy toffees
3 tbsp milk
3 x 100g bars dark chocolate, broken into small pieces, melted
½ tsp sea salt flakes

1 Heat oven to 180C/160C fan/gas 4. Line a 20 x 30cm tin with baking parchment. Whizz the base ingredients in a food processor. Knead briefly to a dough. Press into the base of your tin and bake for 25 minutes until golden. Cool.

2 For the peanut layer, melt the butter and peanut butter in a pan. Stir in the icing sugar. Immediately smooth over the base. Chill for 2 hours to set.

3 For the caramel layer, put the caramel and salt in a pan and boil for 2–3 minutes, whisking continuously, until the colour darkens and the caramel thickens. Cool for 20 minutes, then pour over the peanut layer and chill for 2 hours.

4 For the choc-toffee top, melt the toffees and milk in a small pan and gently heat until they turn into a runny sauce.

5 Pour the melted chocolate over the caramel layer. Drizzle over the toffee, sprinkle over the sea salt flakes and chill for 2 hours.

PER SLICE (20) 502 kcals, protein 8g, carbs 48g, fat 31g, sat fat 16g, fibre 1g, sugar 36g, salt 0.7g

Mini baked cheesecake bites

Everyone's favourite dessert is now bite-size! This simple-to-make traybake can be cut into little fingers for the ultimate sweet canapé.

TAKES 1 HOUR 25 MINUTES ● MAKES 48 LITTLE BITES

250g/9oz gingersnap biscuits
100g/4oz butter, melted
250g tub ricotta
250g/9oz cream cheese
200g/7oz soured cream
3 large eggs
250g/9oz caster sugar
1 tbsp cornflour
1 tsp vanilla extract
finely grated zest and juice from
　1 lemon
150ml/¼ pint double cream
2–4 tbsp lemon curd

1 Heat oven to 160C/140C fan/gas 3. Line the base and sides of a 20 x 30cm shallow tin with baking parchment. Put the biscuits into a food processor and whizz to crumbs. Pulse in the butter, until well mixed. Tip into the tin and spread out evenly. Using the back of a metal spoon, press the mixture down firmly.

2 Clean the food processor and add the ricotta, cream cheese, soured cream, eggs, caster sugar, cornflour, vanilla extract, lemon zest and juice. Whizz until smooth, then pour into the tin. Bake for 40 minutes until the mixture is lightly set. Cool to room temperature.

3 Whisk the cream to soft peaks. Spread over the top of the cheesecake and chill overnight.

4 To serve, remove the cheesecake from the tin and peel the paper from the sides. Cut into 48 small squares or bars. Put the lemon curd into a small disposable piping bag. Snip off the end and pipe zigzags on the cheesecakes.

PER BITE 120 kcals, protein 1g, carbs 10g, fat 8g, sat fat 5g, fibre none, sugar 8g, salt 0.2g

Clotted cream & raspberry ripple Arctic roll

Remember this retro classic? It will go down a storm with your guests.

TAKES 1 HOUR, PLUS FREEZING •
SERVES 15

FOR THE MIDDLE

100g punnet raspberries, squashed
   with the 2 tbsp jam
600g tub vanilla ice cream, out of the
   freezer for 30 minutes
300g jar raspberry jam, minus 2 tbsp
   for the raspberries

FOR THE SPONGE

4 large eggs
125g/4½oz golden caster sugar, plus
   extra for sprinkling
125g/4½oz self-raising flour, sifted

1 Line a 900g/2lb loaf tin with cling film. Ripple the squashed berries through the softened ice cream. Spread in the tin and freeze overnight.

2 Heat oven to 190C/170C fan/gas 5. Line a 25 x 35cm tin with baking parchment. Whisk the eggs and sugar until pale and fluffy – about 5 minutes. Fold in the flour. Spread in the tin and bake for 10–12 minutes until springy.

3 Lay out a large sheet of parchment and sprinkle it with sugar. Flip on the sponge, and loosely roll it up from one of the short ends, with the parchment inside. Cool.

4 Remove the ice cream from the freezer. Transfer it to a large sheet of parchment, then roll it in the paper and shape into a cylinder, 25cm long.

5 Unroll the sponge, then spread with the remaining jam. Sit the ice cream in the centre and wrap the sponge around it. Roll it back up in the parchment, then re-freeze for 2 hours more, until solid.

PER SERVING 372 kcals, protein 5g, carbs 38g, fat 22g, sat fat 13g, fibre 1g, sugar 33g, salt 0.2g

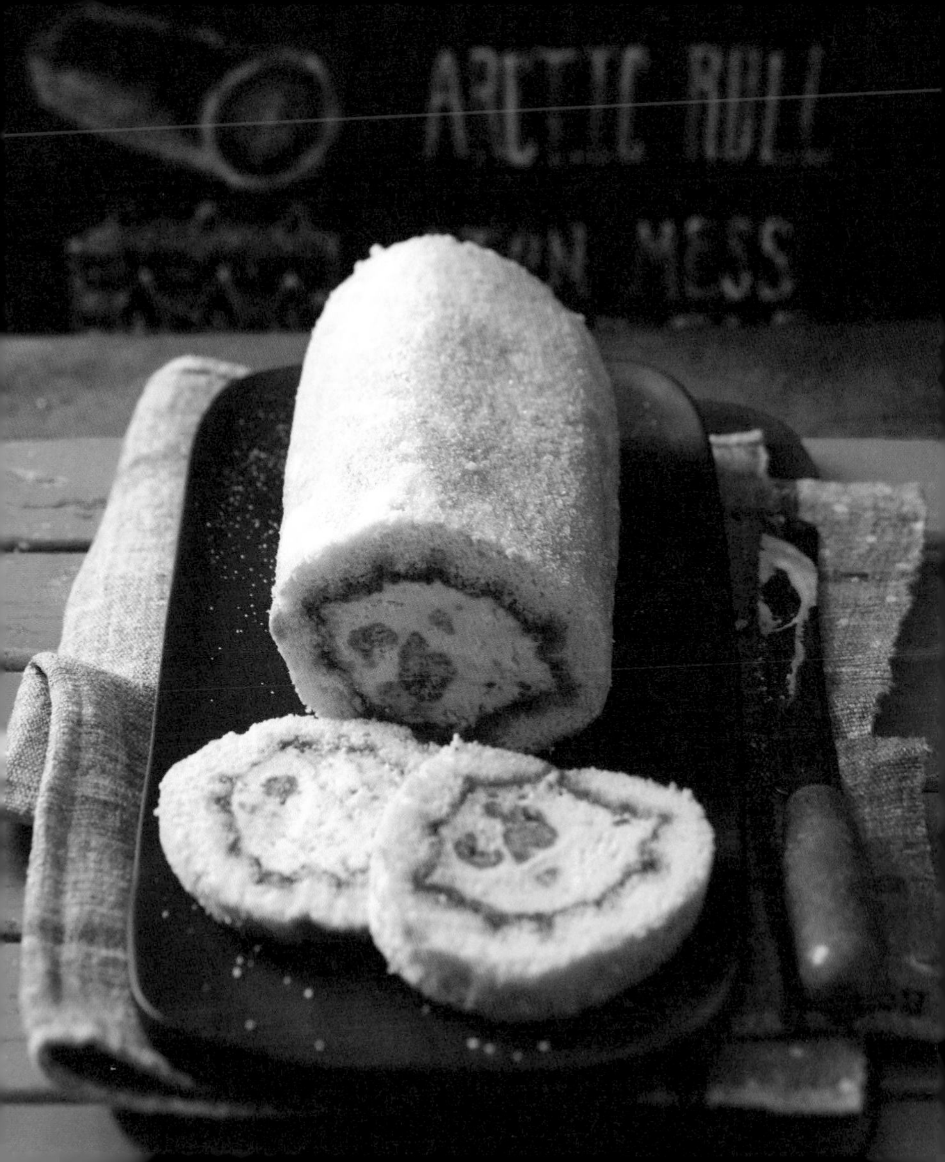
ARCTIC ROLL
MESS

Pear parkin pudding

The addition of sweet baked pears elevates traditional ginger parkin to a whole new level. Perfect for finishing off an autumnal Sunday lunch.

TAKES 1 HOUR 25 MINUTES ●
SERVES 8

140g/5oz butter, plus extra for greasing and dotting over
200g/7oz porridge oats
200g/7oz self-raising flour
2 tsp ground ginger
¼ tsp salt
175g/6oz treacle
140g/5oz light muscovado sugar, plus a little extra
2 balls stem ginger from a jar, chopped, plus syrup to serve
1 large egg
150ml/¼ pint milk
4 ripe pears, peeled, stalks cut off, cored and halved
custard, ice cream or Greek yogurt, to serve

1 Heat oven to 160C/140C fan/gas 3. Butter a 30 x 20cm tin. Mix the oats, flour, ground ginger and salt together. Melt the treacle, butter and sugar together in a large saucepan, then stir in the dry ingredients, half of the chopped ginger, the egg and milk to give a smooth batter.

2 Spoon into the tin, then sit the pear halves in the batter. Dot more butter over each pear half and sprinkle with a little more sugar. Bake for 1 hour until risen all over and a skewer inserted into the middle of the pudding comes out clean.

3 To serve, scatter the rest of the ginger over the fruit, then drizzle all over with syrup from the jar. Serve in rectangles with custard, ice cream or Greek yogurt.

PER SERVING 538 kcals, protein 9g, carbs 81g, fat 22g, sat fat 13g, fibre 5g, sugar 45g, salt 0.91g

Ginger flapjacks

Don't think you can beat a traditional flapjack? Think again. This version has added crunch from desiccated coconut and is then topped with a spiced fudge icing.

TAKES 45 MINUTES ● CUTS INTO 16 SQUARES

250g pack butter, plus extra
   for greasing
200g/7oz light muscovado sugar
5 tbsp golden syrup
200g/7oz porridge oats
100g/4oz whole oats
140g/5oz plain flour
50g/2oz desiccated coconut

FOR THE ICING

175g/6oz butter
200g/7oz icing sugar
4 tbsp golden syrup
2 tbsp ground ginger
few chunks crystallised ginger, diced

1 Heat oven to 200C/180C fan/gas 6. Butter and line a 20–21cm square baking tin with baking parchment. Gently melt together the butter, sugar and syrup in a large pan. Tip in the oats, flour and coconut, and mix well. Press the mixture into the tin to flatten evenly. Bake for 30 minutes until golden and crisping.

2 To make the icing, put the butter, icing sugar, syrup and ground ginger in a small pan and heat gently, stirring, until all melted together. Pour straight over the flapjacks, scatter with the diced ginger and cool in the tin before cutting into squares.

PER SERVING 456 kcals, protein 4g, carbs 52g, fat 25g, sat fat 16g, fibre 3g, sugar 34g, salt 0.5g

Lighter spiced carrot cake

This cake is sure to impress, because once your guests are reaching for their second slice – you can reveal it's healthy!

TAKES 1 HOUR, PLUS COOLING ●
CUTS INTO 15 SQUARES

125ml/4fl oz rapeseed oil, plus a little extra for greasing
300g/10oz wholemeal flour
2 tsp baking powder
1 tsp bicarbonate of soda
1 tbsp mixed spice
100g/4oz dark soft brown sugar
140g/5oz carrots, grated
140g/5oz sweet potatoes, peeled and grated
200g/7oz sultanas
2 large eggs
4 tbsp agave syrup
juice 2 oranges

FOR THE ICING

200g/7oz quark
50g/2oz fromage frais
3 tbsp icing sugar, sifted
zest 1 orange

1 Heat oven to 180C/160C fan/gas 4. Grease and line a 20 x 30cm traybake tin with baking parchment. Mix together the flour, baking powder, bicarbonate of soda, spice and sugar in a big mixing bowl. Stir in the grated carrots, sweet potatoes and sultanas.

2 In a jug, whisk together the eggs, rapeseed oil, agave syrup and juice from 1 orange. Tip the wet ingredients into the bowl and stir to combine, then scrape into the tin. Bake for 25–30 minutes until a skewer poked in comes out clean.

3 Prick all over with a skewer and drizzle over the remaining orange juice. Cool in the tin.

4 Once cool, make the icing. Stir the quark with a spoon to make it a bit smoother, then fold in the fromage frais, icing sugar and orange zest. Spread all over the cake and slice into squares.

PER SQUARE 269 kcals, protein 6g, carbs 38g, fat 10g, sat fat 1g, fibre 3g, sugar 25g, salt 0.4g

Peppermint petticoat tails shortbread

A posh afternoon tea isn't complete without a tray of pretty homemade shortbread.
If you like yours plain, just leave out the peppermint.

TAKES 45 MINUTES • SERVES 8

250g/9oz butter, softened
100g/4oz caster sugar
½ tsp peppermint essence
250g/9oz plain flour, plus extra for
   dusting
100g/4oz cornflour
½ tsp salt
icing sugar, for dusting

1 Put the butter, sugar and peppermint essence in a food processor and whizz until pale and creamy. Add the flour, cornflour and salt, and pulse until the mixture clumps together into small pieces. Tip onto a lightly floured work surface and bring the dough together as a ball, but don't overwork it. Roll out the dough to line a 22cm loose-bottomed square tin, or 25cm round tin, about 1cm thick. Use 2 fingers to crimp all the way around the edge of the dough then, using a fork, mark dotted lines to portion the shortbread into shapes or wedges. Chill for at least 30 minutes.
2 Heat oven to 180C/160C fan/gas 4. Cook the shortbread for 25 minutes until golden and cooked through. Leave to cool completely on the tray. To decorate, place a lacy doily over the shortbread and dust with a generous layer of icing sugar. Pull the doily away to reveal the beautiful lacy pattern. Keep in a tin for up to 5 days.

PER SERVING 445 kcals, protein 3g, carbs 48g, fat 26g, sat fat 16g, fibre 1g, sugar 15g, salt 0.8g

Mango & passion fruit roulade

Your guests will never guess, but this tropical roulade is incredibly low in fat – only 3g a slice!

TAKES 35 MINUTES • CUTS INTO 10 SLICES

3 large eggs
85g/3oz golden caster sugar, plus 1 tbsp
85g/3oz plain flour, sifted
1 tsp baking powder, sifted
1 tsp vanilla extract

FOR THE FILLING

1 tbsp golden caster sugar
flesh from 2 large, ripe passion fruit
2 mangoes, peeled and cut into small chunks
250g pack frozen raspberries, defrosted
200g tub 2% Greek yogurt or very low-fat fromage frais

1 Heat oven to 200C/180C fan/gas 6. Grease and line a 30 x 24cm shallow tin with baking parchment. Put the eggs and sugar into a large bowl and beat with electric beaters until thick and light, about 5 minutes. Fold in the flour and baking powder, then the vanilla. Tip into the tin, tilt to level the mix, then bake for 12–15 minutes until golden and just springy.

2 Turn onto another sheet of paper, dusted with 1 tablespoon caster sugar. Roll the paper up inside the sponge, then leave to cool completely.

3 Fold the sugar, passion fruit pulp and one-third of the mango and raspberries into the yogurt. Unroll the sponge, spread with the filling, then roll up again. Serve with the rest of the fruit on the side. The roulade can be filled and rolled up to 2 hours before serving and kept in the fridge.

PER SERVING 153 kcals, protein 5g, carbs 28g, fat 3g, sat fat 1g, fibre 2g, sugar 21g, salt 0.26g

Little lemon-tons

*If you love a lemon drizzle cake, you'll love these even more, because after cutting
your traybake into squares, every single side gets coated in crunchy lemon sugar!*

TAKES 55 MINUTES • MAKES 16

175g/6oz butter, softened
140g/5oz caster sugar
140g/5oz self-raising flour
50g/2oz ground almonds
½ tsp baking powder
2 large eggs
1 tsp vanilla extract
juice 3 lemons, zest of 2
200g/7oz granulated sugar

1 Heat oven to 180C/160C fan/gas 4.
Line the base and sides of a 20cm
square tin with baking parchment (the
easiest way is to cross 2 x 20cm strips
over the base). Beat the butter, caster
sugar, flour, almonds, baking powder,
eggs, vanilla, lemon zest and the juice
from half a lemon with an electric whisk
until smooth. Scrape into the tin and
bake for 25–30 minutes until a skewer
poked in comes out clean. Cool.
2 Turn out onto a wire rack, trim the
edges and slice into 16 squares. Tip the
granulated sugar onto a plate and pour
the remaining lemon juice into another
shallow dish. Very, very quickly, dip all
sides of the cake squares, one-by-one,
into the juice, then immediately into the
sugar. Sit on a wire rack to set and crisp.

PER SQUARE 299 kcals, protein 3g, carbs 37g,
fat 15g, sat fat 8g, fibre 1g, sugar 29g, salt 0.4g

Blueberry swirl cheesecake

These baked cheesecake bars can be eaten any time of the day – which is a good excuse as one certainly won't be enough!

TAKES 1 HOUR 20 MINUTES, PLUS COOLING • CUTS INTO 14 BARS

300g/10oz digestive biscuits, whizzed to crumbs
140g/5oz butter, melted
275g/10oz golden caster sugar
100g/4oz blueberries
1 tsp cornflour, mixed to a paste with 1 tbsp water
3 x 300g packs full-fat cream cheese
4 tbsp plain flour
2 tsp vanilla extract
3 large eggs
200ml pot soured cream

1 Heat oven to 200C/180C fan/gas 6. Line a 20 x 30cm tin with baking parchment. Mix the crumbs and butter. Press down firmly into the base of the tin, then bake for 10 minutes. Cool.

2 Meanwhile, bubble 25g/1oz of the sugar, the blueberries and the cornflour paste in a small pan until saucy. Cool.

3 Whisk the cream cheese with an electric whisk until smooth. Whisk in the remaining sugar, flour, vanilla, eggs and soured cream until smooth.

4 Pour half the cheesecake mixture over the base, then blob half the blueberry sauce on top. Smooth over the remaining cheesecake. Drizzle the top with the remaining blueberry sauce, then use the end of a spoon to ripple. Bake for 10 minutes, then lower the heat to 110C/90C fan/gas ¼ and bake for 30 minutes. Cool in the oven for 1 hour with the door closed, then leave for 1 hour more with door ajar. Chill overnight.

PER BAR 606 kcals, protein 6g, carbs 39g, fat 47g, sat fat 28g, fibre none, sugar 24g, salt 1g

Pear & cardamom tart

Don't just keep cardamom for curries. Squash pods with a rolling pin, then collect the little seeds inside and finely grind them in a pestle and mortar.

**TAKES 2 HOURS, PLUS CHILLING •
SERVES 8**

500g/1lb 2oz sweet shortcrust pastry
plain flour, for dusting
4 small ripe pears
squeeze lemon juice
drizzle honey, to serve

FOR THE CARDAMOM FRANGIPANE

200g/7oz butter, softened
200g/7oz caster sugar
140g/5oz ground almonds
100g/4oz self-raising flour
50g/2oz toasted flaked almonds, plus
    extra for sprinkling
1 tsp ground cardamom
2 large eggs

1 Roll out the pastry on a lightly floured surface to line an 18 x 28cm tin. Lift the pastry into the tin, prick the base with a fork and chill for 30 minutes.

2 Heat oven to 200C/180C fan/gas 6. Line the pastry with greaseproof paper and fill with baking beans. Bake for 15 minutes. Remove the beans and paper and bake for a further 10 minutes until the pastry is biscuity. Lower oven to 160C/140C fan/gas 3, and trim the pastry edges.

3 For the frangipane, beat the ingredients together with an electric whisk. Spread into the tin.

4 Peel, halve and core the pears – scoop out the core with a melon baller, if you have one. Brush with lemon juice and arrange in the tin, pushing them a little into the frangipane. Scatter with more flaked almonds and bake for 50 minutes until the filling is firm to the touch. Serve warm or cold, drizzled with a little honey.

PER SERVING 833 kcals, protein 12g, carbs 78g, fat 55g, sat fat 21g, fibre 4g, sugar 43g, salt 0.81g

Blueberry lemon cake with coconut crumble topping

This sticky, crumbly bake is irresistible. A great bake to take on a picnic, as the crumblier it gets on the way, the better!

TAKES 1 HOUR • MAKES 16 SQUARES

300g/10oz butter, softened, plus extra
 for greasing
425g/15oz caster sugar
zest 1 lemon
6 eggs, beaten
250g/9oz self-raising flour
300g/10oz blueberries
200g/7oz desiccated coconut
200g/7oz lemon curd

1 Heat oven to 180C/160C fan/gas 4 and grease and line a 20 x 30cm cake tin. Beat together 250g/9oz of the butter with 250g/9oz of the sugar and the zest until fluffy. Gradually beat in 4 of the eggs. Fold in the flour and a third of the blueberries, then spoon into the tin. Flatten with a spatula, sprinkle over another third of the blueberries and bake for 25 minutes until the surface is set.

2 To make the topping, melt the rest of the butter, then stir in the coconut and remaining sugar and eggs until combined. Warm the lemon curd gently for a few minutes in a small pan until it is runny and pourable.

3 After the initial baking, scatter the remaining blueberries over the top of the cake, drizzle over the lemon curd, and crumble over the coconut mixture. Bake for a further 20–25 minutes until golden. Cool in the tin. Cut into squares.

PER SQUARE 446 kcals, protein 5g, carbs 50g, fat 27g, sat fat 17g, fibre 3g, sugar 34g, salt 0.55g

Battenberg

If you've never made a Battenberg before, you might be surprised at how easy it is. There's no need to buy a special tin, a standard square tin will do the job.

TAKES 1 HOUR 10 MINUTES •
SERVES 8

FOR THE SPONGE

175g/6oz really soft butter
175g/6oz golden caster sugar
3 medium eggs
50g/2oz ground almonds
140g/5oz self-raising flour
½ tsp baking powder
½ tsp almond extract
pink food colouring

TO DECORATE

icing sugar, for dusting
500g pack white marzipan
100g/4oz apricot jam, warmed and
    sifted

1 Heat oven to 180C/160C fan/gas 4. Push a snug-fitting foil-covered strip of cardboard down the centre of a 20cm square tin, then line each half with baking parchment. Beat the sponge ingredients (except the food colouring) until smooth. Spread half into one side of the tin. Mix some food colouring into the remaining mixture, then spread into the other half of the tin. Bake for 25–30 minutes. Cool.

2 Trim the sides of each cooled cake, then halve them both lengthways.

3 Dust a clean work surface with icing sugar. Roll a quarter of the marzipan to 20 x 10cm. Brush with jam, then sandwich on one plain and one pink sponge, with jam in between. Brush the tops with more jam, and sandwich the remaining sponges on top.

4 Roll out the remaining marzipan to 20 x 25cm. Brush more jam over the outsides of the cake. Cover with marzipan, trim the excess and crimp the edges to seal.

PER SERVING 652 kcals, protein 8g, carbs 85g, fat 31g, sat fat 13g, fibre 1g, sugar 72g, salt 0.7g

Lime & ginger bars

These are a tropical twist on the classic lemon bars, but with these there's no need for a homemade biscuit base, instead we cheat with crunchy gingernuts!

TAKES 50 MINUTES • MAKES 14 BARS

FOR THE BASE

85g/3oz unsalted butter, melted, plus extra for greasing

250g/9oz gingernut biscuits, crushed finely

FOR THE FILLING

25g/1oz plain flour

200g/7oz white caster sugar

2 large eggs, plus 1 yolk

zest of 2 limes, juice of 4 (you will need 100ml/3½fl oz juice)

1 Line an 18 x 23cm baking tin with foil, then grease the foil lightly. Heat the oven to 180C/160C fan/gas 4 and put in a baking sheet.

2 Mix the biscuit crumbs and butter until even, then press into the bottom of the tin. Press and smooth with the back of a spoon to compact the mix as firmly as you can. Slide the tin onto the warmed baking sheet and bake for 20 minutes, until very dark golden all over.

3 Meanwhile, make the filling. Stir the flour and sugar together, make a well in the middle, then work in the eggs until smooth. Stir in the lime zest and juice. Pour the filling onto the hot base, return to the oven and turn the heat down to 160C/140C fan/gas 3. Bake, still on the baking sheet, for 20 minutes or until set to the middle. Cool on a wire rack, then remove from the tin, peel away the foil and cut into bars.

PER SERVING 200 kcals, protein 2g, carbs 29g, fat 9g, sat fat 5g, fibre 1g, sugar 21g, salt 0.2g

Bacon & ricotta oven-baked frittata

This thickly baked omelette works as a filling supper or can be sliced into wedges and served in lunchboxes or at picnics.

TAKES 40 MINUTES • SERVES 4–6

knob butter
2 leeks, trimmed and sliced
8 rashers back bacon, fat removed
    and chopped
6 large eggs, beaten
250g pack ricotta
100ml/3½fl oz single cream
small bunch chives, snipped
salad and crusty bread, to serve

1 Heat oven to 200C/180C fan/gas 6. Line a 20 x 30cm pie tin with baking parchment. Melt the butter in a frying pan and cook the leeks for 8–10 minutes until soft, adding a splash of water if they start to stick, then tip into a bowl. Add the bacon to the pan and fry for 5 minutes until crisp. Add to the leeks and leave to cool.

2 Add the eggs, ricotta, cream and chives to the leeks and bacon, mix well and season. Pour into the lined tin and cook for 20–25 minutes until set. Serve with some salad and crusty bread.

PER SERVING (6) 267 kcals, protein 18g, carbs 2g, fat 21g, sat fat 9g, fibre 1g, sugar 2g, salt 1.9g

Herby focaccia

There's nothing quite like a homemade loaf of bread. It's time to master this Italian classic; made from scratch the flavour twists are endless.

TAKES 2 HOURS, OVER 3 DAYS
- **SERVES 6–8**

2 x 7g sachets dried active yeast
500g bag strong white bread flour
1 tbsp sea salt, plus extra for sprinkling
75ml/2½fl oz olive oil, plus extra for
   oiling, kneading and brushing
4 rosemary sprigs
4 thyme sprigs
a few bay leaves

1 Mix the yeast with 100ml/3½fl oz hand-hot water in a small bowl. Leave for 5 minutes until bubbling.

2 Add the flour to a bowl and pour in the yeast mix, salt, oil and add 250ml/9fl oz hand-hot water. Mix to a dough, then knead for 10 minutes. Leave for 1 hour in an oiled bowl, covered with oiled cling film to rise. Leave in the fridge overnight.

3 Heat oven to 220C/200C fan/gas 7. Press the dough into a deep, oiled, 20 x 30cm baking tin. Break half the herbs into small bits and push into the dough. Cover and leave until doubled in size.

4 Press holes into the dough with your fingers. Brush with oil and sprinkle with sea salt. Put a shallow tin half-filled with water in the bottom of the oven. Bake the bread on the shelf above for 25 minutes. Scatter over the remaining herbs and bake for another 10–15 minutes until cooked. Cool on a wire rack.

PER SERVING (8) 301 kcals, protein 7g, carbs 45g, fat 9g, sat fat 1g, fibre 2g, sugar 1g, salt 1.9g

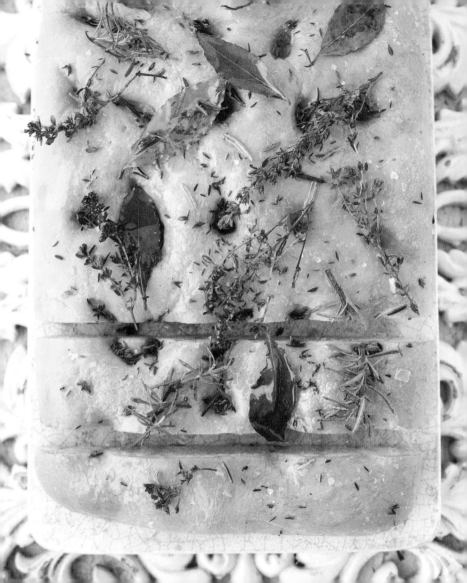

Tuna & sweetcorn slice

Kids will love this cheesy bake – and it should easily stretch to six or eight portions if you are feeding small mouths.

TAKES 35 MINUTES • SERVES 4

320g pack ready-rolled puff pastry
185g can tuna in spring water, drained and flaked
325g can sweetcorn, drained
3 tbsp crème fraîche
50g/2oz Cheddar, grated
a few chives, snipped to short lengths

1 Heat oven to 220C/200C fan/gas 7. Unroll the pastry and lay it into a roughly A4-sized baking tin. Pinch up the edges to form a border, pressing the pastry firmly into the corners. Prick the centre all over with a fork and pop in the oven for 10–15 minutes.

2 Meanwhile, mix the tuna and sweetcorn in a bowl and season.

3 Remove the pastry from the oven, pressing the centre down with the back of a fork, as it will have puffed up a bit. Spread the crème fraîche across the centre, spoon the tuna mix on top, then sprinkle over the cheese. Bake for 10–15 minutes more, until golden, puffed up and cooked through. Sprinkle with chives and cut into portions.

PER SERVING 463 kcals, protein 18g, carbs 29g, fat 30g, sat fat 16g, fibre 1g, sugar 2g, salt 2.6g

Big bacon & egg pie

A bacon & egg pie is a favourite in New Zealand and Australia, where it makes a good brunch, lunch or supper dish.

TAKES 1 HOUR 10 MINUTES • CUTS INTO 15 SQUARES

1.25kg/2lb 12oz shortcrust pastry
plain flour, for dusting
1 egg, beaten
1 tbsp sesame seeds

FOR THE FILLING

12 rashers thick-cut smoked back
  bacon, diced
1 tbsp sunflower oil
4 onions, diced
½ tsp ground mace
2 x 290g jars whole roasted peppers
  in brine
large bunch parsley, finely chopped
10 large eggs (as fresh as you can get)

1 For the filling, gently fry the bacon in the oil in a large frying pan. Turn up the heat to brown the meat. Remove to a plate, then add the onions and mace to the pan. Gently cook until softened. Cool.
2 Line the base and sides of a 20 x 30cm baking tin with baking parchment. Roll out 750g/1lb 9oz of the pastry on a lightly floured surface until big enough to line the base and sides of the tin.
3 Put a baking sheet in the oven and heat to 200C/180C fan/gas 6. Spread the onions on to the pastry base, then open out each pepper flat and use to cover the onions. Scatter over the bacon, then the parsley. Crack over the eggs and season.
4 Roll out the remaining pastry to cover, pinch and trim the edges to seal and brush with the beaten egg. Scatter with sesame seeds. Sit the tin on top of the baking sheet and bake for 30–40 minutes until golden and crisp. Cool at room temperature before serving sliced.

PER SQUARE 510 kcals, protein 14g, carbs 40g, fat 33g, sat fat 10g, fibre 3g, sugar 3g, salt 1.9g

Pinwheel pizzas

Both kids and adults alike will love these pizza-flavoured bites. They are delicious just as they are or served warm spread with butter alongside steaming tomato soup.

TAKES 45 MINUTES, PLUS RISING
● **MAKES 8**

olive oil, for greasing
500g pack bread mix
flour, for dusting
50g/2oz mature Cheddar, grated

FOR THE FILLING

4 tbsp tomato purée
handful basil leaves, roughly torn
1 whole roasted pepper, from a jar, cut into strips
70g pack pepperoni, chopped
125g ball mozzarella, torn into chunks

1 Oil a 22–24cm-square baking tin and line the base with baking parchment. Make up the bread mix according to the pack instructions.

2 Turn out the dough onto a lightly floured surface and roll out to an oblong 35 x 22cm using a rolling pin.

3 Spread the tomato purée over the dough (leaving a border of dough plain all the way round), then scatter over the basil, pepper, pepperoni and mozzarella.

4 Carefully and firmly roll up the dough from the longest side to make a Swiss roll, then slice the log evenly into eight thick pinwheels. Arrange them flat in the tin, a little apart to allow for rising. Cover the tin with cling film and leave in a warm place until the dough is well risen.

5 Heat oven to 240C/220C fan/gas 9. Remove the cling film, scatter the Cheddar over the pinwheels and bake for 12–15 minutes until golden.

PER PIZZA 271 kcals, protein 12g, carbs 31g, fat 11g, sat fat 5g, fibre 1g, sugar 1g, salt 1.3g

Butternut–ricotta tart with fiery rocket salad

Even the most carnivorous members of your family will gobble up this easy vegetarian supper in no time. If you like a punchier cheese, swap some ricotta for goat's cheese.

TAKES 1 HOUR 5 MINUTES • SERVES 4

1 butternut squash (about 600g/1lb 5oz), peeled and cut into 2cm/¾in cubes
2 tbsp olive oil
320g sheet ready-rolled puff pastry
250g tub ricotta
a few sage leaves, finely chopped
good grating nutmeg
zest and juice ½ lemon
70g bag rocket leaves
1 red chilli, deseeded and finely chopped
25g/1oz pine nuts

1 Heat oven to 220C/200C fan/gas 7. Put the squash in a roasting tin, toss in half the oil, season and spread out into a single layer (you may need 2 tins). Roast for 30–35 minutes or until tender.

2 Meanwhile, line an A4-sized traybake tin with baking parchment. Unroll the pastry and lay it in the tin. Score a border around the edge of the pastry with the tip of a knife and prick the inside part all over with a fork. Bake for 15 minutes.

3 Mix the ricotta, sage, nutmeg, lemon zest and plenty of seasoning in a bowl. Once the pastry and squash are cooked, remove from the oven. Gently press the centre of the pastry case down with the back of a spoon to flatten. Spread the ricotta mix into the centre then lay on the squash. Bake for a further 10–15 minutes until the pastry is golden and crisp. Mix the lemon juice, rocket, chilli, pine nuts and remaining oil. Scatter half over the tart and serve the rest on the side.

PER SERVING 577 kcals, protein 14g, carbs 49g, fat 36g, sat fat 14g, fibre 3g, sugar 7g, salt 0.8g

Sicilian pizza

This is a recipe for Sfincione from Sicily – a thick, flavoured bread that is topped with breadcrumbs to give it a crunch once it's baked.

TAKES 2 HOURS • SERVES 6

FOR THE DOUGH

2 x 7g sachets fast-action yeast
2 tsp caster sugar
200ml/7fl oz warm water
375g/13oz strong white bread flour,
    plus extra for dusting
½ tsp salt
1 tbsp olive oil, plus extra for oiling

FOR THE TOPPING

2 pork sausages, preferably fennel-
    flavoured, skins removed then
    crumbled
4 tbsp good-quality tomato sauce
4 tbsp ricotta
6 slices provolone cheese, cubed
2 tbsp dried breadcrumbs
drizzle olive oil

1 Mix the yeast and sugar with the warm water. Put the flour and salt in a mixer with a dough hook, or in a large mixing bowl, make a well in the middle and pour in the liquid and oil. Mix for 5 minutes in the mixer until the dough is silky. Tip into an oiled bowl, cover and put somewhere warm until doubled in size.

2 Tip onto a lightly floured work surface and knead for 2 minutes.

3 Dust a 25 x 16cm traybake tin with flour and put the dough in the centre. Push the dough to the edges of the tin. Leave to rise for 30 minutes. Meanwhile, fry the sausagemeat in a dry pan until crumbly.

4 Heat oven to 230C/210C fan/gas 8. Spread tomato sauce over the dough base and sprinkle over the sausage, ricotta, provolone and breadcrumbs. Drizzle with olive oil. Bake for 5 minutes, then cook at 200C/180C fan/gas 6 for 20–25 minutes, until golden. Cool slightly, then cut into six chunks and serve.

PER SERVING 470 kcals, protein 20g, carbs 52g, fat 20g, sat fat 8g, fibre 2g, sugar 3g, salt 2g

Full English frittata

A frittata is an Italian classic that works really well with everything we Brits enjoy for breakfast – and is perfect for using up leftovers.

TAKES 45 MINUTES ● SERVES 4

8 eggs
50g/2oz soured cream
2 tsp olive oil, plus extra for greasing
4 rashers bacon, cut into strips
12 button mushrooms, sliced
4 leftover cooked chipolatas, cut into
    bite-size pieces
6 leftover roast potatoes, cut into
    bite-size chunks
fresh bread and brown or tomato
    sauce, to serve

1 Heat oven to 180C/160C fan/gas 4. Beat the eggs with a whisk in a bowl, then whisk in the soured cream and some seasoning. Set aside.
2 Heat a non-stick pan, add the oil, then fry the bacon and mushrooms until caramelised and cooked through. Towards the end, toss in the leftover sausages and roast-potato chunks, and allow them to heat up in the pan alongside the bacon and mushrooms.
3 Tip the contents of the pan into a small, lightly greased traybake tin, then pour over the egg mixture. Bake for 20–25 minutes until the egg has risen slightly and set. Serve with fresh bread and brown or tomato sauce – choose your favourite.

PER SERVING 442 kcals, protein 24g, carbs 22g, fat 29g, sat fat 9g, fibre 2g, sugar 1g, salt 1.79g

Cavolo nero & pancetta tart

This lovely lunch or supper dish can be made a day in advance. Keep it somewhere cool, though not in the fridge or the pastry might become soggy.

TAKES 1 HOUR • SERVES 6

500g pack all-butter shortcrust pastry
1 small head cavolo nero (about 200g/7oz), stalk trimmed and leaves separated
70g pack sliced pancetta
200ml/7fl oz whole milk
150ml/¼ pint double cream
2 eggs, plus 1 yolk
85g/3oz Parmesan, grated

1 Heat oven to 200C/180C fan/gas 6. Roll out the pastry and line a deep 20 x 30cm loose-bottomed tart tin. Prick the base and line with greaseproof paper and baking beans. Sit the tin on a baking sheet and bake for 15 minutes. Remove the beans and paper, and bake for a further 5–10 minutes until pale golden.
2 Lower oven to 180C/160C fan/gas 4.
3 Cook the cabbage in a pan of lightly salted boiling water for 4–5 minutes, until tender. Cool, drain well, then squeeze out the excess water. Pat dry with kitchen paper.
4 Arrange the cabbage and pancetta in the tart case. Beat together the milk, cream and eggs until well blended. Stir in the Parmesan, season, then pour into the tart. Bake for 25 minutes until just set.
5 Cool for 10 minutes in the tin, cut into six slices and serve warm, or cold the next day.

PER SERVING 665 kcals, protein 19g, carbs 36g, fat 51g, sat fat 28g, fibre 3g, sugar 4g, salt 1.45g

Salmon & broccoli lattice tart

Using only six ingredients, this salmon tart is super-simple to prepare, but the pastry-lattice top makes it look really special.

TAKES 50 MINUTES ● SERVES 4

100g/4oz broccoli, cut into florets
85g/3oz watercress, chopped
4 tbsp half-fat crème fraîche
425g pack ready-rolled puff pastry
    sheets
1 egg, beaten
170g pack poached salmon fillets,
    flaked
green beans, to serve

1 Cook the broccoli in boiling water until tender. Drain and rinse in cold water until cool. Drain well and set aside. In a food processor, blitz the watercress and crème fraîche with some seasoning.

2 Heat oven to 200C/180C fan/gas 6. Unroll the pastry sheets. Use one to line an A4-size traybake tin. Cut out a 2cm/¾in-wide border from the second sheet, like a picture frame, and stick this onto the first sheet with some of the beaten egg. Prick the base all over with a fork. Bake for 10 minutes until golden.

3 Cut the remaining pastry into 2cm/¾in-wide strips. Spread the cooked pastry with the watercress crème fraîche, scatter with the flaked salmon, broccoli and seasoning, and top with the strips of pastry, arranged to create a lattice effect.

4 Brush the pastry strips with beaten egg and cook for 20–25 minutes until the pastry is golden and cooked through, and the filling is hot. Serve with green beans.

PER SERVING 566 kcals, protein 19g, carbs 32g, fat 41g, sat fat 15g, fibre 2g, sugar 2g, salt 1.23g

Quiche Lorraine frittata

You should have almost all these ingredients, or similar, to hand, so when the sun shines there's simply no excuse not to enjoy a last-minute picnic.

TAKES 45 MINUTES • SERVES 6

8 rashers smoked streaky bacon or about 175g/6oz ham, chopped into pieces
8 eggs
200ml/7fl oz milk
50g/2oz strong Cheddar, grated, plus extra for sprinkling (optional)
soft bread rolls, cherry tomatoes and salad leaves, to serve

1 Heat oven to 180C/160C fan/gas 4. If you're using bacon, put it into a large frying pan and cook over a gentle medium heat. Stir occasionally until golden and beginning to crisp.

2 Line a roasting tin, about 20 x 28cm, with baking parchment – just scrunch it roughly at the corners. Whisk together the eggs and milk in a large jug or bowl, then stir in the bacon or ham, plus any fat from the pan, the Cheddar and some seasoning. Pour into the tin, scatter with a bit of extra grated cheese, if you like, and bake for 30–35 minutes until golden and set.

3 Carry to your picnic in the tin and eat hot, warm or cold, sandwiched in bread rolls, with cherry tomatoes and a few salad leaves.

PER SERVING 229 kcals, protein 17g, carbs 2g, fat 17g, sat fat 6g, fibre none, sugar 2g, salt 1.3g

Cheesy spinach bake

This makes a great lunchbox filler for all ages. Pack up small squares for children with a handful of cherry tomatoes, and add a leafy green salad for grown-ups.

TAKES 1 HOUR • CUTS INTO 6–8 SLICES

200g pack feta
2 x 250g tubs ricotta
3 x 100g bags baby leaf spinach, chopped
bunch spring onions, finely sliced
50g/2oz Parmesan, grated
1 egg
good grating nutmeg
100g/4oz breadcrumbs
2 tbsp olive oil
6 sheets filo pastry

1 Heat oven to 180C/160C fan/gas 4. Mash the feta in a large mixing bowl, then add the ricotta and mash again to thoroughly mix. Stir in the spinach, spring onions, Parmesan, egg, nutmeg and plenty of seasoning with half the breadcrumbs.

2 Brush a 20 x 30cm baking tin with a little oil. Layer in half the filo sheets, brushing each one with oil before topping with another. Scatter the remaining breadcrumbs evenly over the base. Spoon in the ricotta filling and gently spread, so as not to dislodge the breadcrumbs.

3 Cover with the remaining filo, brushing with oil as you go, then score into portions. Bake for 35–40 minutes until golden and crisp. Eat cold or warm.

PER SLICE (8) 436 kcals, protein 23g, carbs 32g, fat 25g, sat fat 13g, fibre 2g, sugar 5g, salt 2g

Quick chilli cornbread

This low-fat cornbread is the perfect accompaniment to a chilli con carne or a big bowl of spicy soup.

TAKES 55 MINUTES • CUTS INTO 8 SQUARES

butter, for greasing
300g/10oz fine semolina or polenta
85g/3oz plain flour
2 tsp bicarbonate of soda
1 large egg
150ml/¼ pint milk
425ml/¾ pint buttermilk or natural yogurt
2 large red chillies, deseeded and finely chopped

1 Heat oven to 190C/170C fan/gas 5. Generously butter a 25 x 16cm baking tin. Combine the semolina or polenta, flour and bicarbonate of soda in a large bowl and season well.

2 In a jug, combine the egg, milk, buttermilk or yogurt and chillies. Pour the contents of the jug into the bowl of dry ingredients and stir lightly to combine. Do not over-stir as this will cause the bread to be tough.

3 Pour the batter into the tin and bake in the oven for 35–40 minutes until firm and golden on top. Cut the warm cornbread into 8 squares to serve. Serve immediately or leave to cool then reheat, wrapped in foil. Can be frozen for up to 1 month.

PER square 198 kcals, protein 8g, carbs 39g, fat 2g, sat fat 0.7g, fibre 1g, sugar none, salt 1g

Smoky cheese & onion tart

This glorious tart has much of the flavour of a good quiche but is much easier to assemble.

TAKES 1 HOUR 5 MINUTES • SERVES 6

6 rashers smoked bacon, chopped
small knob butter
3 onions, thinly sliced
200ml/7fl oz double cream
500g block shortcrust pastry
plain flour, for dusting
140g/5oz hard farmhouse cheese,
    such as Cheddar, half grated,
    half crumbled
1 egg, beaten
140g/5oz cherry tomatoes, halved

1 Heat oven to 220C/200C fan/gas 7. Sizzle the bacon in the butter for 6 minutes until just starting to crisp. Add the onions and sweat for 10 minutes until sticky and golden. Add the cream and leave to cool slightly.

2 Meanwhile, roll out the pastry on a lightly floured surface to a rectangle a little larger than A4 and transfer to a baking sheet. Roll up the edges a little and press them over onto the pastry to create a raised border.

3 Mix the onions with the grated cheese and most of the egg. Spread over the pastry, then top with the tomatoes and crumbled cheese. Brush the edges with egg, then bake for 20 minutes until golden. Cool and cut into squares to serve.

PER SERVING 759 kcals, protein 18g, carbs 47g, fat 57g, sat fat 27g, fibre 3g, sugar 6g, salt 2.32g

Red onion & rosemary focaccia

This is a nice, quick dough to make and shape – perfect for first-time bakers.

TAKES 1 HOUR, PLUS RISING

• CUTS INTO 8 SQUARES

500g/1lb 2oz strong white flour, plus extra for dusting

7g sachet fast-action yeast

5 tbsp olive oil

about 350ml/12fl oz lukewarm water

sunflower oil, for greasing

2 large red onions, sliced

handful rosemary sprigs

1 tsp sea salt flakes

1 Tip the flour, yeast and a pinch of salt into a large bowl. Make a well in the middle and pour in 2 tablespoons of the olive oil and most of the water. Use a wooden spoon to mix together to a slightly wet dough – add a splash more water if necessary.

2 Tip the dough on to a lightly floured surface and knead for 10 minutes until smooth and elastic. Put in a clean oiled bowl, cover with oiled cling film and leave to rise until doubled in size.

3 While the dough is rising, cook the onions in 1 tablespoon olive oil until soft.

4 When the dough has risen, knead for 30 seconds, then stretch to fit an oiled 25 x 35cm baking tin. Cover with a tea towel and leave to prove for 20 minutes.

5 Heat oven to 200C/180C fan/gas 6. Spread the onions and rosemary over the dough. Press your fingers into the dough to make dimples, drizzle the remaining oil over and scatter over the sea salt. Bake for 30 minutes until golden.

PER SQUARE 297 kcals, protein 8g, carbs 51g, fat 8g, sat fat 1g, fibre 2g, sugar 3g, salt 1.13g

New potatoes Lorraine

This clever recipe gives you all the flavour of the well-loved Quiche Lorraine but none of the fiddly pastry lining. Instead it's been transformed into an easy traybake.

TAKES 50 MINUTES • SERVES 4

650g/1lb 7oz baby new potatoes
1 tsp olive oil
2 shallots, thinly sliced
200g/7oz thick smoked bacon rashers, chopped
4 large eggs
300ml/½ pint milk
170ml pot double cream
100g/4oz Cheddar or Gruyère, or a mix of both, grated
handful rocket leaves, plus your favourite salad dressing, to serve

1 Heat oven to 180C/160C fan/gas 4. Boil the potatoes for 10–12 minutes until almost tender.

2 Meanwhile, heat the oil in a frying pan and fry the shallots and bacon until the shallots have softened. Beat the eggs, milk and cream with some seasoning.

3 Slice the potatoes thickly – you can skin them first, if you like – and put in a large, shallow ovenproof dish.

4 Scatter over the bacon and shallots over the potato slices, then pour over the egg mixture and scatter on the cheese. Bake for 25–30 minutes until set. Serve scattered with dressed rocket.

PER SERVING 650 kcals, protein 27g, carbs 28g, fat 48g, sat fat 25g, fibre 3g, sugar 6g, salt 2.8g

Pea & spring-onion tart

This light quiche is delicately flavoured and delicious. Save it for summer when you can serve up slices of it in the garden.

TAKES 1 HOUR 20 MINUTES

● **CUTS INTO 12 SQUARES**

FOR THE PASTRY

200g/7oz plain flour, plus extra for dusting

100g/4oz butter, chopped

50g/2oz mature Cheddar, finely grated

FOR THE FILLING

bunch spring onions, sliced

25g/1oz butter

200g/7oz frozen peas

150ml/¼ pint milk

3 large eggs

200g/7oz crème fraîche

good grating nutmeg

100g/4oz mature Cheddar, grated

1 Heat oven to 200C/180C fan/gas 6. Pulse the flour and butter in a food processor to fine breadcrumbs. Pulse in cheese to combine. Add 2–3 tablespoons cold water and mix to a firm dough.

2 Knead briefly, then roll out on a lightly floured surface and line a 30 x 20cm rectangular tin with the pastry. Chill for 15 minutes. Cover with greaseproof paper, fill with baking beans and bake for 10 minutes. Remove the paper and beans, then bake for 10 minutes more until biscuity. Trim the excess pastry.

3 Reduce oven to 180C/160C fan/gas 4. Fry the spring onions in the butter gently until softened. Add the peas, season and cook gently for 5 minutes. Whizz in the food processor with the milk to a purée.

4 Beat the eggs with the crème fraîche, nutmeg, half the cheese and the pea purée. Pour into the pastry case, sprinkle with the remaining cheese. Bake for 25–35 minutes until the filling is firm.

PER SQUARE 287 kcals, protein 8g, carbs 15g, fat 22g, sat fat 13g, fibre 2g, sugar 2g, salt 0.5g

Salmon & lemon-rice pastry parcel

This slice is so versatile: great warm for supper, with new potatoes and a green salad, or served cold for a picnic (leave it in the tin for easy transportation!).

TAKES 50 MINUTES, PLUS CHILLING
● **CUTS INTO 6 SLICES**

3 medium eggs, 1 lightly beaten
250g pouch ready cooked lemon
   basmati rice
3 tbsp low-fat crème fraîche
small bunch parsley, chopped
1½ tbsp capers, rinsed and chopped
4 spring onions, sliced
3 hot-smoked salmon fillets (about
   225g/8oz), skin removed, flaked
100g/4oz ready-roasted red peppers
   from a jar, drained and chopped
plain flour, for dusting
500g pack all-butter puff pastry

1 Boil 2 of the eggs in a small pan of water for 8 minutes. Cool under cold running water, then peel and quarter.
2 In a large bowl, mix the rice, crème fraîche, parsley, capers, spring onions, salmon and peppers. Season well.
3 On a lightly floured surface, divide the pastry roughly in half, with one piece slightly larger than the other. Roll out the slightly larger piece to line a baking tin about 25 x 20cm. Spoon the rice mixture on top, then nestle in the egg quarters. Roll out the remaining pastry, lift on top and pinch the edges together to seal. Trim any excess pastry. Chill for 15 minutes. Meanwhile, heat oven to 220C/200C fan/gas 7.
4 Brush the parcel all over with beaten egg and make a small slit in the top. Bake for 25 minutes until golden and hot through. Serve warm or cold, cut into 6 slices.

PER SLICE 514 kcals, protein 19g, carbs 42g, fat 30g, sat fat 13g, fibre 1g, sugar 2g, salt 1.5g

Ham & asparagus toad-in-the-hole

Everybody loves a traditional toad-in-the-hole with crispy sausages, but come summer try this lighter, seasonal version.

TAKES 30 MINUTES ● SERVES 4

16 thick asparagus spears
2 tbsp vegetable oil
2 eggs
140g/5oz self-raising flour
150ml/¼ pint milk
2 tbsp chopped mixed herbs, such as
    parsley, dill and oregano
8 slices lean ham, halved
crunchy green salad, to serve

1 Heat oven to 220C/200C fan/gas 7. Cook the asparagus spears in boiling salted water for 2 minutes, drain and set aside on kitchen paper.
2 Pour the oil into a 37 x 26.5cm shallow roasting tin and put in the oven to heat up. Whisk the eggs, flour, milk and 150ml/¼ pint cold water together until smooth, or whizz in a food processor. Season and stir in the herbs.
3 Wrap each asparagus spear in a piece of ham. Arrange them in the hot roasting tin and pour over the batter. Bake for 20 minutes, or until risen and golden. Serve with a seasonal salad.

PER SERVING 288 kcals, protein 19g, carbs 28g, fat 12g, sat fat 3g, fibre 3g, sugar 4g, salt 1.84g

Index

Also available from BBC Books and *Good Food*